Toward

BETTER
HUMAN
RELATIONS

Toward

BETTER
HUMAN
RELATIONS

LLOYD ALLEN COOK, *Editor*

*Holder of the Leo M. Franklin Memorial Chair
in Human Relations at Wayne University
for the Year 1950-51*

Essay Index Reprint Series

 BOOKS FOR LIBRARIES PRESS
FREEPORT, NEW YORK

STANDARD BOOK NUMBER:
8369-1284-5

LIBRARY OF CONGRESS CATALOG CARD NUMBER:
70-90626

PRINTED IN THE UNITED STATES OF AMERICA

PREFACE

THIS VOLUME presents the first annual Leo M. Franklin Lectures in Human Relations, a product of the Chair in Human Relations established at Wayne University by Temple Beth El, Detroit, as a memorial to Dr. Franklin.

Dr. Franklin was rabbi at Temple Beth El from 1899 to 1941, when he became emeritus. He died in 1948. During his ministry, he served one of the largest and most influential congregations in the nation. He did not, as his late successor, Dr. B. Benedict Glazer, has said, "pursue a parochial pastorate." On the contrary, he was a loyal and faithful servant of every worthwhile, humanitarian cause. He was an indefatigable worker for better human relations, including the welfare of racial and creedal minorities.

As first holder of the Franklin Memorial Chair, I am deeply grateful to the Temple, its officials and congregation; and to President David D. Henry, Dean Clarence Hilberry, and the Wayne University faculty. I would, if it were possible, share this award with my associates in the College Study in Intergroup Relations, all the persons named and unnamed in a two-volume final report cited in Chapter 5. It was as director of this Study that I came to appreciate more fully the iron curtains which separate us as races, creeds and classes, weakening us for the tasks of world leadership in which our lot is cast.

As to the lectures in this volume, they were given at the

University as public addresses. Each speaker was selected as a distinguished leader in his field. Dr. Louis Wirth, who died May 3, 1952, was a sociologist. He speaks in this lecture of freedom, power and value issues, defining some of the problems which the nation faces. Dr. Eduard C. Lindeman, a social philosopher, follows with a conception of democracy which would, in essence, subject its basic claims and presuppositions to scientific test. The next lecture, the one by Gordon W. Allport, a social psychologist, is a critical discussion of methods in current use to resolve intergroup tensions. It seemed appropriate at this point to turn to ameliorative action, starting with Dr. Dorwin Cartwright's presentation of the group dynamics approach to the problem of changing people. Until Kurt Lewin's death, Cartwright was associated with him in group dynamics research. The last lecture, by the editor, an educational sociologist, consists mainly of concrete cases from College Study files which illustrate some ways of working with people on tensional issues. These are followed by a brief consideration of intergroup education as a study-action field.

I have regretted very much the need to shorten some of the papers. Aside from adding center headings, my editorial work has been slight. I wish to acknowledge the assistance of Alexander Brede and other officials of the Wayne University Press. To the following publishers, and to Robert Bierstedt, author, it is a pleasure to express gratitude for permission to quote: American Association of Collegiate Registrars and Admissions Officers, American Council on Education, American Council on Race Relations, Beacon Press, and the Macmillan Company, Harper and Brothers, and Charles Scribner's Sons.

It should be added that this publication has been made possible by a recent grant from Temple Beth El.

LLOYD ALLEN COOK

Detroit, May, 1952

CONTENTS

Toward Better Human Relations

CHAPTER 1

Freedom, Power and Values in Our Present Crisis

LOUIS WIRTH

Professor of Sociology, University of Chicago; formerly Director of the American Commission on Race Relations.

LOUIS WIRTH

Freedom, Power and Values in Our Present Crisis

I SHOULD LIKE TO EXPRESS MY APPRECIATION of the honor of opening this annual lecture series under auspices of the Leo M. Franklin Chair in Human Relations at Wayne University. May I express the hope, in which those who will follow me in this series will, I am sure, be glad to join, that the expectation of building a living monument to a great preacher and practitioner of human relations will be realized.

The subject assigned to me is so broad in scope that it permits me to roam at will over the universe of ideas and ideals. On one thing I think we can easily agree, namely, that we as a people and as a nation, and the world in which we live, are in a grave crisis. The Chinese, if we may still draw lessons from them, are reported to have a way of writing the word *crisis* by two characters, one of which signifies "danger," the other "opportunity." If we will remember the former, it will save us from being complacent. If we recall the latter, it may save us from becoming hysterical. Besides acknowledging that we live in a state of crisis, if we would be of help in dealing with it, the least we can do is to analyze the nature of the dilemma, plus the dangers and opportunities with which it confronts us.

WORLD POLARIZATION OF POWER

The crisis in which we live is a phase of a profound historic upheaval. Like all crises it has its roots in the fact that an existing equilibrium has been upset and that the form of the new equilibrium, which is emerging, cannot as yet be foreseen. This disequilibrium is on a world scale. Forces have come into play which threaten the status quo and which are shaking our institutions, our habits, our norms, and our expectations.

What makes the present crisis so dramatic is the fact that the world has been polarized by two great concentrations of power and ways of life. At one pole is the United States; at the other, the Soviet Union. No such large scale polarization of power has ever existed in the world. In the face of this fission and the tensions to which it has given rise, some peoples may seek security through neutrality. But we know and they suspect that if and when these centers of power come to grips, the ensuing struggle will encompass the world and will permit no neutrals. Under the circumstances the temptation may be great to resign from the human race; but, alas, there is no other crowd to join.

We cannot hope to find a way out of this crisis by merely proclaiming our self-righteousness and the wickedness of our adversary. It helps us little to divide the world into the "free" world and the "slave" world, especially when such arduous efforts are under way to enlist on the side of the free those whom only lately we felt to be in the camp of the tyrants, and when on the side of the unfree there are aligned hundreds of millions of people who are no less human than we, peoples for whom we have professed great sympathies and who have lately been our allies.

Nor does it help us much to divide the world into the peace-loving and the war-like peoples. Such a cliche will be turned against us in the end, for we know deep in our hearts that the masses of people everywhere would prefer peace to war. Such a glib dichotomy is not likely to rally to our cause those whom we seek to enlist; nor is it likely to demoralize those who are our potential enemies.

Rather than indulge in such forms of self-deception, we might more profitably inquire into the basis of the conflict between the two great power systems which threatens to erupt into a world conflagration or else to smolder for years and leave the world impoverished and divided into two armed camps. Surely it cannot be that it is merely or primarily the co-existence in the world of two divergent economic systems, the private enterprise and the collectivist, for there is room for both, and there are already many variations and gradations of the two. Nor can it be the mere co-existence of two political ideologies which tears the world asunder, for we must admit that political ideologies have come and gone throughout history. Moreover, if we really believe democracy to be on the march and to be superior to totalitarianism, which the Russians and their satellites call· by the euphonious name of "Peoples' Democracy," thus paying at least lip service to democracy, the superiority of one system over the other cannot be settled by force of arms. There was a time in the history of the western world when a parallel crisis arose with the rise of Protestant-ism as a heretical doctrine, when many people felt that the two creeds and churches could not exist side by side. Despite the religious wars, it has turned out that not only they but other religions can compete freely for adherents by relatively peace-ful means.

We have lately been told that it is not Soviet communism, but rather Russian expansionism or imperialism, which underlies and produces the world's tragic predicament. If this be true, it calls for measures, peaceful if possible and backed by collective force if necessary, to restrain imperialistic aggression. To give way to the fatalistic doctrine that armed conflict between the two power centers is inevitable, however, can only lead in the end to making it inevitable. *Ideas can only be fought by ideas.* Economic systems can only be preserved in the face of counter systems by demonstrating their ability to yield more beneficent results. It is only when ideas and economic systems become coupled with great concentrations of military power, so that they no longer maintain themselves in the face of opposition on the basis of their merits, that they constitute a danger to peace.

FACTORS OPERATING AGAINST PEACE

I do not mean to suggest that a mere wish on our part that sweetness and light prevail in the world will alter the grim situation in which we find ourselves. There are four factors at work which operate against the peaceful settlement of differences and the peaceful co-existence of two great powers. The first is the fact of the iron curtain, which calls attention to *the break-down of communication.* Soviet censorship and insularity have inhibited not only the communication of our leaders with the Russian leaders, but the communication of our people with the Russian people. Under these circumstances, the exchange of information, mutual persuasion by rational means and demonstration, based on personal experience of the merits or demerits of the respective systems of society and of the truth or falsity of the claims made for each by its proponents, have virtually ceased. Even where the will to free communication still exists it is inhibited in action through the operation on the Russian side of what amounts to a worldwide conspiratorial organization in the form of the international communist parties. Through these nuclei in various countries Russia has been able to use the citizens of other countries as its own agents for carrying out espionage, sabotage, and the undermining of morale. Unfortunately, one of the counter-moves, on the part of the various nations of the world, including the United States, designed to protect themselves against such corrosion from within, has been to erect a western counterpart to the iron curtain. The total effect of this has been either to drive what inter-communication exists underground or to stop it altogether. As a result, we may only expect mutual ignorance, misunderstanding, and suspicion. As Mr. Churchill said recently, "It is difficult to say whether the Russians today do not fear our friendship more than our hostility."

Another factor complicating international relations is the cumulative effect of fear, especially *the legitimate need for defense against aggression.* However justified the action of one country to defend its national interests may be, it is interpreted by the other as an aggressive gesture. It is countered by a defensive action that is interpreted by the country against which it is directed as an aggressive measure. Thus defense and aggression operate in a vicious circle to heighten tension and bring it to the exploding point. Weakness on one side serves as an invitation to the other to exercise its strength, which leads in turn to counteraction to overcome the weakness. This interplay of gestures—even if initially neither nation was bent upon aggression—is bound, if not effectively halted, to lead to disaster.

A third factor standing in the way of a peaceful solution of differences is *our own lack of clarity concerning the values which we seek to preserve and to enhance.* Without a clear understanding of what our values are and a corresponding conviction concerning the need to defend them, we cannot formulate a sound national policy. From the evidence provided by current studies of public opinion it is safe to conclude that the American people are confused about the objectives of national policy and hence have only the vaguest and most contradictory notions about the legitimacy of the sacrifices that are demanded of them. In the struggle for the minds of men, we do not seem to know clearly what to say to the world. Our adversaries, however brazenly and hypocritically, do.

A fourth factor contributing to our vulnerability is *the great disparity between our resources and the poverty of most of the rest of the world*. Although we constitute only about 7 per cent of the world's people, we produce about 60 per cent of the world's industrial products. But our wealth and material prosperity are not the most impressive aspects of our civilization. In the eyes of the impoverished peoples of the world, they are just as likely to arouse envy as admiration. Irrespective of the many good things that we have done and are doing, millions of people just awakening to national self-consciousness and moving out from under the domination of colonial regimes regard us, together with the European powers that once ruled over them, as imperialists and exploiters. It will take time and resolute action to persuade them to the contrary.

SAFEGUARDING OUR LIBERTIES

Precisely because we have such vast material resources upon which to build our power, we are likely to underestimate, and others are unlikely to see, the non-material aspects of our civilization. It will not appreciably enhance our status among the peoples of the world to boast of our might and our riches. These have been widely enough advertised. The world knows much less about our ideals and what we are doing to realize them. Millions of people have been led to believe that our professed democracy is but a sham. In answer to the charge that political freedom in America is extinct we may point to the record in recent years of the United States Supreme Court in reasserting and protecting our fundamental liberties. An effective answer to the charge that we are the slaves of Wall Street, is to point to the fact that we have over fifteen million workers organized into free trade unions, who, although they enjoy higher standards of living than any similar group of workers in the world, are free to negotiate and if necessary to strike and to carry on political agitation for further improving their status. The best answer to the charge that our public opinion is regimented, is to point to the fact that in 1948 a Presidential candidate, in the face of almost unanimous opposition from press and radio, staked his political life on the issue of civil rights, and won.

One of the gravest dangers confronting America in the present crisis is the trend and pressure toward conformity. In combatting the forces that seek to undermine our national integrity we may fall into the trap of so circumscribing our freedoms as to make the difference between ourselves and our adversaries seem indistinguishable. The drift toward suppressing deviational heresy is ominous. The "subversive" label can silence even the most justified criticism and the most legitimate protest. The tendency to impose special oaths, to institute purges, to deprive men of their vocations and to destroy their careers on the basis of rumor and guilt by association, has no foreseeable limits. The gravest danger of all is that to the pressure from without we will add a pressure from within, namely, *the disposition to engage in self-censorship*. Unless these tendencies are promptly reversed it is to be feared that responsible criticism will become extinct and that intellectual stupor will settle over the land.

THE NEED TO DEFINE BASIC VALUES

Obviously we cannot hope to formulate, much less to pursue, our vital national interests effectively unless we have a clear conception of our fundamental values. The clarification of these values and the determination of where we stand with reference to them becomes, therefore, one of the most imperative tasks to be faced by us as a people and as a world power. Similarly, if we are to play our role as a world power effectively, it becomes important for us to know what are the basic values which are cherished by other nations and to what extent these values are similar to and different from our own. We would probably find that despite many local and national differences the masses of men have much in common. As Charles H. Cooley put it: "Always and everywhere men seek honor and dread ridicule, defer to public opinion, cherish their goods and their children, and admire courage, generosity, and success. It is always safe to assume that people are and have been human."[1] It is not in these life objectives but rather in the means regarded as appropriate for their realization and in the priority that circumstances give to different values that important distinctions are likely to be found.

In a recent inquiry which UNESCO undertook among intellectuals from various countries, it was found that almost no one failed to profess acceptance of democracy as a value. It was equally obvious, however, that the specific content which persons ascribed to the concept and the emphasis they put upon some its ingredients differed considerably. While the importance of these findings should not be exaggerated, it is clear that democracy as a value has found such wide acceptance throughout the world that undemocratic societies have appropriated

[1]Charles H. Cooley, *Social Organization* (New York: Charles Scribner's Sons, 1909), p. 28.

the term for propaganda purposes while rejecting its implications for policy.

It seems highly probable that what is true of democracy is true of other symbols representing the values of men. This seems to call attention to an important obligation which scholars and social scientists might undertake, namely, to penetrate beyond the symbols and, through empirical studies, to ascertain the specific content of the values in which people profess to believe and to determine the actual values by which they live. It would probably be found that even where the values of different societies or different groups within the same society seem to be superficially identical, the priority which is given to certain values as over against others, the means which are regarded as legitimate for their attainment, and the sacrifices which people are willing to make to realize their values would throw a great deal of light on the conflicts that divide our world. Such an analysis would probably furnish a better guide for action than we now have, especially if we further analyzed these values in the light of the social problems which different peoples regard as the most urgent.

The atmosphere in which we live, however, is not conducive to such dispassionate analysis. Before we regard violent conflict as inevitable, it would be well for us to remember that even if we fought a war against the Russians to a victorious end, the problems which produced it would still demand solution. These problems are the poverty and misery of a great part of the world, the great inequalities of opportunity within and between peoples, the lack of personal freedom and security, the absence of the rule of law and of respect for the dignity and significance of human beings. The task of organizing and developing the resources of the world for the benefit of its peoples would still remain. Hence the possibility of finding alternatives to violent world conflict through diplomacy, through the agencies of the United Nations and through keeping open every avenue by which we might reach agreements that could be accepted with honor, must remain an article of faith on the part of men of good will everywhere.

A prerequisite for such a just and peaceful resolution of international tension is the recognition that the particular institutional forms in which our highest values find expression are perhaps not the only forms, and that other people must choose for themselves the appropriate embodiment of their most cherished values in the light of their history and needs. If the search for a mutually acceptable *modus vivendi* is to succeed, we must be on guard not merely against naivete, complacency and treachery, but also against our own ethnocentrism, self-righteousness, and hysteria. Above all, if we are to retain our loyalty to our own ideals of freedom, of equality of opportunity, and of respect for the significance and dignity of man, and if we are to win and retain the respect and confidence of the great masses of common people throughout the world, we must actively practice what we profess to believe both at home and in our relations with other nations. We must unhesitatingly resist the temptation to sell our soul for expedient economic, political or military advantages.

VALUES AND SOCIAL ACTION

We have learned that the most important thing to know about a person is what he takes for granted, and the most important thing to know about a people is what it takes for granted. We have also learned that we cannot always believe what people say, but that what they say is nevertheless important. This suggests that the values by which people live can be more effectively inferred from what they do rather than from what they say. It is our history as a people, rather than merely our formal declarations, that tells us what our values truly are. Our formal pronouncements on these values, however, constitute the guide posts to public policy, the criteria by which we judge our own progress and by which others judge our general goals. These statements of public policy formalize our national creed and awaken our conscience. As a great liberal American stateman, Carl Schurtz, said, "Ideals are like the stars. We never reach them, but like the mariner of the sea, we guide our course by them."

It is the discrepancy between our avowed aims and our actual achievements that, as Myrdal has put it, defines the American dilemma. At no point is the gap between ideals and actuality in American life greater than in the case of *race relations*. In no aspect of our national life are we more vulnerable to criticism. Hence, if we are concerned about enhancing our role of moral leadership in the world, it behooves us to do all in our power to make the American dream become a reality.

Our national creed is embodied in a number of documents expressive of public policy. Most important among these are the Declaration of Independence, the Preamble to the Constitution, the Bill of Rights, the Emancipation Proclamation and the Civil War amendments, the Atlantic Charter, the report of the President's Committee on Civil Rights, recent Supreme Court decisions on restrictive covenants, equality of educational opportunity, and equal access to public facilities and services. Our role in the formulation and adoption of the Charter of the United Nations and the efforts of our representatives in the draft of the Universal Declaration of Human Rights are the most recent expressions of our commitment to an international policy in the light of which we must reexamine our own domestic practices.

What we commonly call the problems of racial and cultural relations are not something separate and apart from our day-to-day living. They consist rather in bringing the various aspects of our life more closely into accord with the values we profess to cherish. Concretely, this means provisions for equalizing opportunities in employment, housing, health, education, recreation, public facilities and services; in the administration of justice, the armed services, and political, religious and social relations. Wherever a segment of our people is set apart from the rest by virtue of their race, creed or national origin, deprived of the opportunities which the others enjoy, subjected to hazards against which others are protected, there we have minorities. The very notion of the existence of minorities in our midst is incompatible with the basic values of American life.

It is obviously futile to attempt to change private, personal prejudices by enacting laws. It is no less futile to attempt to get rid of legally sanctioned segregation by efforts to modify the attitudes of the public officials who are merely the functionaries charged with executing the laws. I have called attention elsewhere[2] to the range of problems of race relations and to the significant differences between some of the problems of race relations such as prejudice, discrimination, segregation, tension, violence and non-integration, and the appropriate methods of dealing with these problems. Suffice it to say here that although prejudice is widely regarded as the central problem of race relations, and though it admittedly is a factor in other problems, such as discrimination and intergroup conflict, prejudice does not seem to be either the most important problem or the one most amenable to treatment. I consider discrimination more significant and more likely to yield to treatment.

[2]Louis Wirth, "Research in Racial and Cultural Relations," *Proceedings of the American Philosophical Society,* 92, No. 5 (1948), 381-386, and "Problems and Orientations of Research in Race Relations in the United States," *The British Journal of Sociology,* 1, No. 2 (1950), 117-125.

Thus it is often argued that the effort to pass laws against discrimination in employment or in education is useless because "you cannot legislate prejudice out of existence." The fact is that in seeking to pass laws against discrimination we are not attempting to use legislation to eliminate prejudice, but rather to eliminate discriminatory actions.

However this may be, it should be pointed out that in a democracy the attempt to enact a law, and the administration of a law, may itself have profound effects in modifying attitudes and shaping behavior. Often, when a specific form of action designed to deal with discrimination is proposed, those who are unwilling to come out openly for the action argue that education is the way to solve the problem. The effect of this argument, and one might even say its intent, often is to prevent any form of action. Without minimizing the importance of education, it may be said that participation in action is often a more effective educative device than either teaching or preaching. The setting up of an actual example in a community as a model to demonstrate equality of opportunity is often more effective as an indirect means of modifying attitudes and behavior than any direct appeal to reason or sentiment or any propaganda seeking to induce people to modify their action. Moreover, modifications in attitude and behavior may often be more effectively brought about through changing a situation than by appealing directly to people to change themselves. The possibility of changing attitudes through the dissemination of factual information is, to say the least, highly limited.[3]

At any rate, in the field of racial and cultural relations, as in other problem areas, it is in the long run more promising

[3]Arnold Rose, *Studies in the Reduction of Prejudice* (Chicago: American Council on Race Relations, 1949) and Robin M. Williams, Jr., *The Reduction of Intergroup Tensions* (New York: Social Science Research Council, 1947).

to follow a scientific approach than a sentimental approach. Although we are far from having the answers to the many questions that confront us in bringing our practices more nearly into accord with our ideals, it is a wholesome sign of the times that an increasing number of trained people are entering the field of race relations and that this professional personnel is increasingly relying upon verified and tested knowledge rather than upon magic, unsystematized common sense, and un-disciplined sentiment as a guide to practice.

AMERICAN LEADERSHIP

In dealing with the rest of the world, and especially with the charges of those who seek to discredit us, it is not only futile but unwise to deny the existence of our internal problems. As the Report of the President's Committee on Civil Rights put it, only a country as strong as ours could afford to acknowledge openly the extent and gravity of its imperfections in realizing the ideals of a democratic society. It is a significant fact that there are over twelve hundred public and private organizations in the United States which are either exclusively, or in some major aspect of their work, concerned with solving the problems of racial and cultural relations. We have gone further than any other nation to acknowledge the existence of our short-comings and to take steps to overcome them.

Fortunately, conditions in the United Staates are such as to constitute a favorable atmosphere in which issues of in-equality of opportunity, of discrimination and tension, can be solved peacefully. Our fundamental laws are conducive to such a solution, and our institutions are flexible. The great regional differences which once divided the country are being minimized. What our minorities want most, namely, *equal justice under the laws and equal opportunities* in employment, housing, edu-cation and public services, our society—even in the South—

can readily grant, without sacrificing any important value. And what some, especially some Southern whites, fear most, namely, that the Negro wants social intimacy with whites, the Negro wants least. We can build upon the progress we have already made to accelerate the pace by which we narrow the gap between our ideals and practices.

In the present state of the world, and considering the role which the United States has been called upon to play, we can ill afford to take lightly the discrepancy between our professed ideals and sober reality. We live in a shrunken world, in which there has taken place a revolution in communication. Through this technological revolution, hitherto backward and isolated areas are experiencing a profound upheaval. Hitherto dormant countries are awakening to national self-consciousness. Along with the right of self-determination, they are also coming to claim the other human rights which in Western history found their dramatic expression in the French and American revolutions. The ideology which inspired the birth of the American nation is arriving at these outposts of the world rather belatedly, but nonetheless imperatively.

Though what is happening in near and far Asia is in many ways linked to communism because of a historic coincidence, it would have had to be dealt with even if the Russians had not, as they undoubtedly have, given it their support. What is not essentially a communist movement can nevertheless be easily exploited by the Communists. The salient fact with which we must reckon is that the ideal of democracy, which we have so assiduously cultivated and diffused among the underdeveloped peoples of the world, *has actually been taken seriously.* To those who consider ideals merely as subjects to be preached rather than practiced, this comes as a surprise or even as a shock. At any rate the content of this ideal has come home to haunt the colonial regimes which still survive and are striving to retain their grip on scores of millions of peoples whose clamor for the privileges of full membership in the human race is an eloquent testimony to the effectiveness of our schools, our missionaries, our traders, our diplomats and propagandists.

Recent experiences should have taught us that friendships and loyal allies cannot be bought by dollars alone. Economic aid is, of course, an indispensable measure in bringing the submerged masses of the world out of the stage where a blind struggle for survival is the dominant force determining their allegiance. Not only will the spirit and action of the benefactor be important in deciding how his assistance will be received, but his relationships with the beneficiary will also be decisive. It will take more than the giving and receiving of material aid between nations to weld the ties of mutual respect and the will to sacrifice. It takes a common cause in the devotion to which neither party can be suspected by the other of ulterior motives. If the United States is to retain the leadership of the world that is struggling toward a fuller measure of freedom and equality, this leadership must be asserted not by rattling a sword, though a sword we must have. It cannot be had by indiscriminate philanthropy and futile bribery, though our aid is urgently needed. It can be achieved by maintaining security and productivity, freedom and justice at home, and by unfalteringly exemplifying these principles in the world at large.

Some may say that in our present grave predicament the measures requisite to a closer approximation to our ideals of a democratic nation and a democratic world must be postponed until a more tranquil moment when we can again afford to take them out of the deep-freeze. Those who counsel us to wait until such a time, however, fail to see that the continuing struggle to translate our ideals into reality is the source of our greatest strength.

CHAPTER 2

Functional Democracy in Human Relations

EDUARD C. LINDEMAN

*Formerly Professor of Social Philosophy,
New York School of Social Work,
Columbia University.*

EDUARD C. LINDEMAN

Functional Democracy

in Human Relations

W̲HENEVER I THINK ABOUT THE LATE RABBI
FRANKLIN, I am reminded of Jane Addams. They both loved
their local communities and labored in behalf of community
improvement. They were both concerned about the deeper
values involved in human deprivation and frustration. Their
liberalism was founded upon the same moral fundamentals,
and they were both fervent exponents of democracy as a living
faith. It seems to me, therefore, appropriate to begin this lecture with one of Jane Addams' pungent statements about
democracy. Years ago, in *The Spirit of Youth* she wrote:

> The doctrine of democracy, like any other of the
> living faiths of men, is so essentially mystical that it
> continually demands new formulations. To fail to recog-
> nize it in a new form, to call it hard names, to refuse to
> receive it, may mean to reject that which our fathers
> cherished and handed on as an inheritance not only to
> be preserved but also to be developed.

For present purposes, I should prefer to alter one of
the words in the above quotation. Instead of saying that

democracy requires continuous reformulation because of its essentially "mystical" quality, I should prefer to say that this necessity arises because of democracy's essentially *dynamic* implications. It is precisely because many of our generation, inheritors of the democratic tradition, have lost contact with the dynamics of democracy that I have undertaken the task of affirming the democratic faith in modern terms.

THE CONSENTING PROCESS

The fanatical dogmas of fascism and communism have maneuvered democracy into a defensive position. As usually happens, when the defensive position is assumed, those who are attacked are betrayed into defense of the past rather than the future. Thus, many ardent believers in democracy are today defending Eighteenth Century democratic ideas and practices. I call this a betrayal since it unconsciously leads many fine citizens to interpret democracy as a conservative rather than a progressive force. But if democracy cannot be promoted as a source of progress, it will automatically falter and fail. If we persist in explaining democracy as a conservative doctrine, we shall play into the hands of communists. We thus gratuitously present them with their most effective arguments, especially in those regions of the world (Asia, for example) where the awakening masses have at last begun to move toward a better life. When contemporary communists call their doctrine Twentieth Century democracy they are obviously being cynical but also clever propagandists.

A simple illustration will, I believe, suffice to demonstrate why democracy must continue to be dynamic and progressive. In the Eighteenth Century when the democratic idea was conceived almost exclusively in political terms, it was assumed that its basic principle was government by consent. The consenting procedure was indeed a simple matter. Issues were discussed in face-to-face town meetings. When a majority was created in favor of a proposition it was thereupon assumed that the problem had been resolved. In our time issues are debated, not in town meetings but in the press, on the radio and through the instrumentality of innumerable propaganda devices, which if known in the past would have been regarded as highly immoral. The consenting process has become so complex that many citizens no longer participate in its political phase. In the last national (Presidential) election, slightly more than half of America's eligible voters took the trouble to cast their ballots. They had abdicated from the consenting process. In many elections we now determine issues, not by true majorities but by majorities of a remnant minority.

Faced with this dilemma, we may respond by insisting that nothing can be done about present complexities. If citizenship becomes too complicated for certain voters, we shall be obliged to accept the consequences of being governed by fictitious majorities. Others may take the position that in modern civilizations it is unrealistic to believe in government by consent. Both of these attitudes, it seems to me, are erroneous and, if followed, will lead to democratic disintegration and decay. There is, however, a third available alternative: we may decide that the machinery of political democracy needs revision. We may, in other words, take a dynamic or progressive position and strive to bring democratic processes up-to-date. And, I repeat, if we are incapable of supporting democracy as a growing, living faith, it will automatically be superseded.

DEMOCRACY, AN EXPANDING THEME

My present task is not historical in mood, but it seems appropriate to insert at least one historical item. The theme of democracy has been nourished from many and diverse sources. Some of its values may be traced to religious beginnings. The notion of personal dignity is, for example, basically a religious conception. The idea of equality appears to stem from mystical sources. Liberty is primarily a political idea, and fraternity as an ideal has both religious and romantic antecedents. Jewish, Greek and Roman thought have each in its turn made significant contributions to the democratic doctrine. One may find distinctively democratic principles in the philosophy of Confucius.

Considered in historical perspective, it is therefore valid to assume that democracy is an eclectic conception. Its values derive from many and variable sources and this fact alone accounts for the non-dogmatic character of the democratic doctrine. It is a doctrine but it is not doctrinaire. It has traceable sources but no single source. It is this fact which also accounts, in part at least, for the important historical conclusion that democracy is both a growing and an expanding idea.

This expansiveness of the democratic idea gives anxiety to some conservatives. Many of this group would prefer to restrain democracy, to keep it, for example, within political bounds. They balk when it is suggested that political democracy needs to be buttressed by economic and cultural democracy. They would feel happier if government, business and culture could, somehow, be kept within separate compartments. They have become accustomed to governmental democracy, but when the notion of equality is expanded, for example, to include racial equality they are confronted with the arduous necessity of changing certain deeply ingrained habits, and this becomes painful. But it is one of the requirements of a dynamic idea that it must continue to expand or wither and die. Insofar as the democratic idea becomes *a way of life,* it must of necessity expand and become applicable to all significant aspects of human existence. This historical imperative places two difficult responsibilities upon believers in democracy. They must, in the first place, prepare themselves for the application of democratic principles to wider and wider ranges of human experience. And, in the second place, and this is even more difficult, they must become sufficiently creative to seek new values to serve as guides for new experiences.

I have called these imperatives difficult, but to me they are also exciting. When democracy is considered as an expanding theme it also becomes adventurous as a way of living. The mere challenge of seeking for new ways of applying democratic values and practices turns experience into an inventive process. The thought of democratic family experience, for example, produces new prospectives regarding individual differences and their role in group life.

THE PROBLEM OF HUMAN RELATIONS

One of the startling and disturbing features of modern life is to be found in the current concentration upon human relations. Why, at this particular juncture of history, should it have become necessary to focus attention upon relations between persons? Why should the task of "getting on with each other" have become so difficult in our age? Or, to pose this question in sharper language, why are we at present aware of the fact that our relations with others have deteriorated? Why widespread anti-Semitism in the mid-Twentieth Century? Why do religious tensions increase and deepen? Why do business concerns now find it necessary or advisable to employ specialists in public relations?

We live in a time of snarling contentiousness. Fanaticism and persecution are common manifestations. We suspect our neighbors. We are no longer content to recognize and discuss points of difference between ourselves and others but are now impelled to utilize derogative labels which put a stop to reasonable communication. Suspicion, anger and finally hatred are the controlling elements in the current context of human relations. Positive toleration tends to be supplanted by negative denial. And thus it happens that sensitive persons have in recent times become aware that soul-searching reflection as well as scientific investigation in the sphere of human relations have become imperative pre-occupations.

It seems appropriate to quote one of these senstitive persons, a scientist, indeed a Nobel Prize winner, and one of the greatest physicists of our time. In the introductory chapter of his book called *The Intelligent Individual and Society,* Professor P. W. Bridgman inserts a most significant confession:

> As I grow older, a note of intellectual dissatisfaction becomes an increasingly insistent overtone in my life. I am becoming more and more conscious that my life will not stand intelligent scrutiny, and at the same time my desire to lead an intelligent, ordered life grows to an almost physical intensity. . . .
>
> I realize that I have only a murky awareness of what is going on. I can ask myself all sorts of questions that I cannot answer, yet which I feel I ought to be able to answer. I am not at all sure that my actions are decently well adapted to procure the ends which I have in view; nor, in the few cases where I attain this moderate degree of self-consciousness, am I at all sure that the ends which I have in view would please me if I could envisage all *relations with other people.*[1]
>
> *The things which bother me most seem to involve my* the consequences. In short, I am not able to answer my questions with regard to my life, whether concerning fact or chance of success, with even an approach to that clearness and completeness which I demand in my scientific activities. . . .

[1] P. W. Bridgman, *The Intelligent Individual and Society* (New York: The Macmillan Co., 1938), pp. 1-2. Italics are mine.

The last sentence has become for me a disturbing refrain: "The things which bother me most seem to involve my relations with other people." Over and over these words repeat themselves and finally a conviction evolves. Gradually I come to realize that it is precisely in this realm of human relations that the deepest and the most puzzling flaw in modern life exists. Together with this conviction arises its counterpart, namely, the determination to devote myself henceforth primarily to this situation and its attendant problems.

CONCEPTIONS OF DEMOCRACY

These convictions have led me to a re-examination of the ideological pattern which by affirmation at least has dominated American experience, namely, democracy. I regard this exercise as a philosophical prelude to a more scientific approach. Those of us who strive to think philosophically must, it seems to me, assume the responsibility of stating as clearly as possible certain propositions which may thereupon become suitable problems for scientific inquiry. At any rate, this is the function which I have assumed.

The democratic idea may be thought of in at least three distinct contexts. It may be regarded as a clue to ways of conducting our associated or communal life. Parliamentary method, trial by jury, the committee system, et cetera, these may be considered as ways of conducting certain public affairs in which conclusions must be reached in spite of conflicting interests and opinions. In this setting democracy may be regarded as a set of social mechanisms. But democracy is also an expanding cluster of ideals proposed by persons who envisage more perfect individuals and more perfect societies. Equality, liberty, fraternity, dignity: these are samples of the ideal content of democracy. And there are, finally, ways of living which stem from democratic experience and which appear in the character of disciplines.

Of these three views of democracy, I shall stress the latter, the idea of disciplines of democracy, on account of two deep-seated convictions. A consideration of disciplines brings the democratic situation into the sphere of science, for disciplines can be taught. Second, if we become more assured in this realm, we should thereupon find workable means for including democracy within our education system. The mechanics of democracy can, of course, be readily taught, but teaching the classical democratic ideals is, however, a more difficult enterprise. The proposition which I wish to state is this: *There is no effective way of teaching ideals unless these ideals are interpreted as the higher reaches of behavior which can be validated in part by tested experience and in part by science.* In other words, an ideological conception which is capable of engaging both our emotional and rational support must be one which can be validated by experience and by science. It must take on the character of an empirical discipline which is believed and acted upon because it is at one and the same time compatible with ideal and practical criteria.

DEMOCRATIC DISCIPLINES

The above paragraph brings us back to the central theme of how democracy may become an implement for improving human relations. In general I am insisting that this end cannot be attained if we merely continue to repeat the classical ideals and exhort people to believe in their worth. The democratic way of life imposes upon its adherents a much sterner obligation. The rituals and slogans of democracy are, no doubt, important but only if buttressed by actual conformations of behavior.

(1) Experience in the democratic way of life has, it

seems to me, demonstrated that under democratic conditions there should never be an expectation of perfect realization of ideals. Democratic solutions, in other words, are always partial, never complete. Perfectionism and democracy are incompatibles.

(2) Democratic experience appears to have demonstrated the fact that diversity is superior to uniformity. *E Pluribus Unum*—through diversity towards unity—produces results which, when measured by humane standards, are better than those which follow upon rules of uniformity. *Gleichschaltung* is antithetical to the democratic ideal.

(3) Democratic experience seems to have provided assurance with respect to the doctrine that the means must, so far as possible, be consonant with the ends. The opposing doctrine which totalitarians espouse, that the ends justify the means, is unscientific before it becomes immoral.

Here, then, are three democratic disciplines which we may utilize as tests for our central proposition. Living toward the democratic ideal implies that we recognize and cherish our individual differences, and that therefore, we accept the responsibility of decent compromise and toleration for diversities. It implies that we assume the obligation of testing every proposal in the light of compatibility between means and ends. And, it requires us to continue the experiment of living without ever anticipating a perfect outcome.

Are these three disciplines internally consistent? Does experimentalism without expectation of a perfect solution conflict with the idea of diversity, or with the notion that means and ends must be compatible? I recognize no logical incoherence in these three disciplines. Indeed, it seems to me that all three are mutually related and represent a re-enforcing trinity. The non-perfectionist does not expect any other individual to be exactly like himself; thus he admits diversity. And precisely because he respects difference in others he also accepts the rule

·that restrains him from exploiting the other person, that is, of using him as a means to some external end.

Are these three disciplines supportable when subjected to the scientific test? I believe so. Non-perfectionism in human affairs seems to me wholly in harmony with the scientific concept of relativity. The rule of diversity pervades the realm of nature and lies at the bottom of all theories of survival. And, science furnishes a most convincing validation for the means-ends doctrine. According to scientific insights it seems indisputable that we become what we do. The assumption that desirable ends may be attained through the use of undesirable means finds no justification in scientific thought.

If these three democratic disciplines are valid in logical as well as scientific terms, how may they be employed on behalf of human relations? I regard these three principles, and I have purposefully restricted myself to only three, as being empirical in character. These are disciplines which have emerged from experience and they possess the added merit of being supportable by science. With so much validity as support, these principles in turn seem to me suitable for moral use. This conjunction furnishes a clue for modern ethics.

Democracy, in other words, when considered in this light becomes a source of value. Values thus derived may be taught with a high sense of integrity and assurance. If we desire an improvement in the realm of human relations, here is our nexus of value. Here are principles which may be taught and exemplified with impunity. The classical democratic values would take on a new lustre and a new realism if these empirical principles were utilized as the means by which we could move closer to our democratic ideals, not merely through verbal affirmations but through practical conditionings of behavior.

What is new about this conception is the proposition that democracy can be taught as a way of life only if its ideal values are sustained by a set of empirical values, values which may be considered to be disciplines of conduct, much in the same manner as Quakers use the word *discipline* as an instructional instrument. It remains now to provide an illustration of my proposal as applied to one of the classical or ideal democratic values, namely, fraternity.

TEACHING THE DISCIPLINES

Liberty, equality and fraternity! It is this trio of values which has, since the French and American revolutions, served as the moral symbol of the democratic struggle. Social philosophers have in the past stressed the first two, liberty and equality, but have strangely neglected the third. It is only now when we have become disturbed about our human relations that the fraternity ingredient in democratic idealism has come to the fore. If the mere incantation of this ideal, if hortatory appeals were effective, we should long since have learned the practice of mutual affection. But the truth of the matter seems to be that the sense of brotherhood has diminished rather than increased. How, then, may those of us who are committed to the democratic way of life acquire the habit of feeling and practicing a persistently affectionate interest in people? How may we, in other language, learn the arts of good human relations?

I now make my appeal on behalf of the three democratic disciplines discussed above. Members of a democratic community should be taught and allowed to practice the rule *of partial functioning of ideals*. Dogmatic and fanatical individuals cannot acquire the art of fraternity. Perfectionism is, indeed, a kind of malformation of personality, an insulating and separating agent. "Not perfection as a final goal," writes John Dewey, "but the ever enduring process of perfecting, maturing, refining, is the true aim in living. . . . The bad man is the man

who, no matter how good he has been, is beginning to de-
teriorate. The good man is the man who, no matter how
morally unworthy he has been, is moving to become better.
Such a conception makes one severe in judging himself and
humane in judging others."[2]

Perfectionists are at the outset handicapped in the realm
of human relations because they, perforce, think of themselves
as superior beings. The perfectionist believes that he knows
what is desirable. He is less interested in what is possible. But
his desired ends can never be realized unless he is prepared
to operate in the context of what is at any given moment
possible. Ah, says the perfectionist, then you want me to betray
my convictions, to become a compromiser, an opportunist! No,
I reply, I want you to hold your "convictions in a high and
worthy spirit" but not to insist that everybody "should be
inspired by the same convictions." I want you to lead a sympathetic life, and if you are to act on behalf of your convictions
and not merely continue their stubborn announcement, you will
be obliged to learn the art of compromise. But there are two
ways of compromising, one which debases and one which leads
forward toward an ideal.

What has been said above about the experimental, as distinguished from the perfectionist way of life, leads directly
to the consideration of discipline Number Two, *diversity*. An
upward-moving compromise takes into account the essential
differences in one's fellows. It is based upon the assumption
that these differences are the elements which distinguish personality. The good compromise is the one which makes use of
the variable qualities in other persons. The bad compromise
is the one which either denies the integrity of interpersonal
differences or accepts subjugation to these differences, thus

[2]John Dewey, *Reconstruction in Philosophy* (New York: Henry
Holt & Co., 1920).

denying one's own distinguishing qualities. Fanatical mass movements are evil precisely on this account: they compel individuals to deny their own persons, to become nonentities. Here again we discover one of the principal sources of corruption in all totalitarian movements whether of the Right or the Left. They ennoble the mass and degrade the individual. Does this doctrine of democratic diversity imply that there is to be no unity? Are we to remain forever in disparate, isolated cells of individualism? The answer to this query, it seems to me, is an emphatic NO. A feeling of unity is a fundamental requirement for normal persons. But, the unity which democracy promises is never achieved through uniformity. It is always "through the many, one," a constant movement in the direction of unity through the creative utilization of diversity. Relations between persons would automatically improve if this discipline were obeyed.

We come finally to the rule which insists that *ends and means must be,* insofar as this is possible in a world inhabited by imperfect persons, *compatible.* I have already intimated that this discipline is validated by both science and morality. This does not mean, however, that it is a simple rule to apply under all circumstances. In the context of our present theme it does mean that democratic goals can never be attained through the employment of non-democratic methods. It implies that good human experience cannot emanate from a relationship in which one person commands and other obeys; from situations in which one person or one group chooses the ends and thereupon uses others as the means. And it implies further that end-gaining individuals, persons who concentrate upon goals, are likely to become careless respecting their means.

Perhaps the wisest comment ever made with respect to the subtle equation of ends and means was that of Ralph Waldo Emerson when he said, "The ends pre-exist in the means."

This is but another way of stating that we become what we do. If we genuinely aim at a society in which there are to exist maximum freedoms, equalities and fraternal associations, we must be constantly alert respecting the methods we employ in all affairs. We may proclaim these beautiful ideals over and over and at the same time conduct ourselves in such manner as to preclude their realization.

At this moment, for example, while we are involved in a gigantic struggle against Communist expansion, it is not unusual to find well-meaning citizens moving towards an abandonment of certain civil liberties, principally to the right of free speech. To the extent that we participate in such betrayal, we too become totalitarians and by our neglect of the proper means play false to democratic principles. If we can combat totalitarianism only by becoming totalitarian, then the battle has already been decided: the totalitarians have won.

*   *   *   *

In this lecture, an attempt has been made to demonstrate the functional relationship between ideals and disciplines of conduct, thus to state a practical conception of morality. Its essence is the proposal that improved human behavior—in our special case, improved human relations—cannot be anticipated if ideals are not supported by rules of conduct which may be validated in part by experience and in part by science. Its further meaning is the proposition that democracy for our time and the future cannot be sustained and preserved unless we become thoroughly self-conscious with respect to its disciplines. Once we become self-conscious concerning our faith in the democratic way of life we thereby create another responsibility, namely, the obligation to make democratic training an integral part of our entire educational system. *Empirical principles are teachable.*

CHAPTER 3

Resolving Intergroup Tensions, An Appraisal of Methods

GORDON W. ALLPORT

Professor of Psychology, Harvard University.

GORDON W. ALLPORT

Resolving Intergroup Tensions,
An Appraisal of Methods

THERE ARE TWO GOOD REASONS why we must expect people to cling tenaciously to their prejudices. For one thing, the whole economy of their lives may be erected on the assumption that certain outgroups are inferior, threatening, or contemptible. Their own sense of worth is maintained by debasing others, particularly groups that are as easily defined as Catholics, Jews, Mexicans, Negroes, refugees. Such people feel safe only on an island with their own kind. Their thinking is categorical: ingroups are good, outgroups, bad; ingroups are safe, outgroups, menacing; ingroups, superior, outgroups, inferior; ingroups, clean, outgroups, dirty. Many lives are organized in this manner. Their economy is one of restriction in human relations. It is not to be expected that such lives can be easily recentered.

A second obdurate fact is that prejudiced attitudes receive continual support from the social environment. While the child may learn fragments of the American creed at school or at church, these fragments are ordinarily smothered by much stronger forces in the environment. To him the sanctions of his home and his gang are much stronger than the sanctions of school or church. No child, for example, can escape the ethnic, religious, and class membership of his parents. If they are the victims of prejudice, he automatically becomes a victim. If prejudice is the parental style of life, it becomes his. How else indeed shall the child survive? While there are certainly contradictory elements in the pattern it is not hard to see where the major emphasis lies for millions of children. Lillian Smith has described vividly the predominant impact that falls on the white Southern child.[1] Since the child's circle of playmates is likely to come from the same ethnic, religious, or social class as himself, their influence usually intensifies the family pressure. Needing the approval of his peers the child does not lightly flaunt their mores.

For such reasons as these, little or no change in prejudiced attitudes can be expected. But there are arguments to be made on the other side, reasons for expecting changes under definable conditions.

Prejudiced attitudes, so far as we know, have no hereditary basis. Young children are disconcertingly democratic. Their sense of the clan comes hard and relatively late. When asked the simple question, "What are you?" only 10 per cent of four-year-olds reply in terms of racial, ethnic, or religious membership; whereas 75 per cent of nine-year-olds do so.[2] Not only is prejudice itself learned, but so, too, are all of its ingredients. And what is learned can, theoretically at least, be unlearned; or at least, the learning can *ab initio* be prevented.

What is more, Americans have an inexhaustible faith in environmentalism. We brush aside the aristocratic biases that

1Lillian Smith, *Killers of the Dream* (New York: W. W. Norton & Co., Inc., 1949).

2E. L. Hartley, *et al.,* "Children's Perception of Ethnic Group Membership," *Journal of Psychology,* 26 (1948), 387-98.

blood will tell, that caste and caste attitudes are imperishable. We believe in the efficacy of education. Psychologists today are obsessed with "learning theory." Advertising is a national idol and we know that to a degree it controls attitudes. With optimism we overhaul our school curricula, launch publicity campaigns, and march forth to slay attitudinal dragons. I am not saying that all this optimism is justified. But our faith in environmentalism itself is a factor of prime importance. If everyone *expects* attitudes to change through re-training, then of course, they are more likely to do so than if no one expects them to change. The very gusto that attends present efforts to reduce prejudice will bring forth maximum results—and the magnitude of these results may yet surprise us.

SOME RESEARCH DIFFICULTIES

Today we have reached a point where we can begin to submit this dispute to empirical tests. Efforts to improve human relations are as old as the hills. What is new in our age is the ability and the will to evaluate the success of these efforts.

Working, as we are, at the frontiers of the subject we do well to keep the principal methodological obstacles clearly in mind.

(1) It is hard to know what indices of change to look for. Thus at the outset we have trouble with our *dependent* variable. If we decide to rely on the measurement of attitudes before and after a program of action, where shall we find scales that are reliable, valid, and not so transparent that the individual gives only the answers he knows the experimenter expects? Even a good scale incurs the criticism that the verbal response it elicits may not correspond at all to conduct in daily life.

(2) It is hard to isolate the program of action that we are testing. Here we run into trouble with our *independent* variable.

Suppose we want to try the effect of a curriculum in intercultural education upon eighth-grade children. How can we make certain the results at the end are not the product of maturation, or exposure to comic books or radio stories, or of a general change in social climate? Even if we prove that the change resulted from the curriculum, how can we tell what features of the program were effective?

(3) It is hard to create satisfactory control groups. Up to now the commonest failing in research has been in the lack of control groups. In Dr. Cook's review of twenty-four recent college programs in intercultural education only four employed controls.[3] It is not easy to find a control population matched with the experimental population for age, intelligence, status, initial prejudice and concurrent experience (in all respects save only exposure to the program itself). Students gossip outside of school about their experience, and thus the control group may be contaminated by the experimental.

(4) It is hard to know when to evaluate the effects of a program. We find it convenient to do so immediately after its close. But the program may have "sleeper effects" and first show its influence months or years later.

There is no need to dwell on the difficulties in this field of research. They are so great that only the most brazen of social scientists will venture to tackle problems of evaluation. But fortunately there are brazen souls, and up to now they have produced not less than 150 evaluative studies. Reviewing this literature, Bierstedt mournfully concludes:

> The findings are bewilderingly diverse. Sometimes there is reported a diminution of prejudice, or at least of adverse opinion; sometimes there is no diminution. Sometimes the conclusion is that prejudice is diminished

[3]Lloyd Allen Cook, ed., *College Programs in Intergroup Relations* (Washington: American Council on Education, 1950).

in this respect but not in that; sometimes the relation is reversed. Sometimes one category of students is reported to be more responsive; sometimes another category.[4]

The problem, we may as well admit, lies at the outer fringe of scientific accessibility, and yet progress is being made. On all sides we encounter the mushrooming of scientific evaluations of social action. Industrial policies are being systematically tested. The efforts of social agencies to prevent juvenile delinquency and to build character are put under the lens of scrutiny. The effects of various styles of college teaching are weighed. And now we have scores of studies pretending to evaluate methods for reducing intergroup tensions.

RESEARCH DESIGN AND CHANGE INDICES

The proper design for experimentation in this field requires the following arrangement:

	Dependent Variable	Independent Variable	Dependent Variable
Experimental Group:	measure of prejudice	exposure to program	measure of prejudice
Control Group:	measure of prejudice	NO exposure to program	measure of prejudice

Needless to say the experimental group and the control group should be matched (equated) in every respect excepting only in their exposure to the independent variable, i.e., to the program intended to change their attitudes.

Virtually all of the strategies employed in the effort to improve group relations can be placed under one of the following six headings, though each could be extensively sub-divided. This list will guide us in our present survey of findings.

[4] In R. M. MacIver, *The More Perfect Union* (New York: The Macmillan Co., 1948), p. 288.

1. Formal educational methods
2. Contact and acquaintance programs
3. Group retraining devices
4. Mass media
5. Legislation
6. Individual psychotherapy

What we want to know is how the above independent variables have presumably affected *knowledge, beliefs, attitudes,* or *behavior* (dependent variables). Unfortunately these four departments of personality are not all one and the same thing. Few investigators are concerned with the differences between them. Yet knowledge may be found to change while behavior remains the same; or beliefs may change but not attitudes. Such inconsistency has been made the subject of a special symposium edited by Chein and others.[5]

For the time being, most investigators are preoccupied in finding a method of measuring change. One cannot be too hard on them for failing to ask *change in what?* After all, a successful measure of any change represents some degree of progress. Eventually we shall have to raise the question whether we are actually measuring a larger portion of the subject's life than our instrument covers. For the moment it is enough to list certain concrete *indices of change.* They alone define what we mean experimentally by the phrase "resolving intergroup tensions." The following list represents an extension of the indices mentioned by Deri and his associates.[6]

(1) *Case studies.* Least quantified but perhaps most convincing are the play-by-play accounts of the introduc-

[5]I. Chein, *et al.,* eds., "Consistency and Inconsistency in Intergroup Relations," *Journal of Social Issues,* 5, No. 3 (1949).

[6]S. Deri, *et al.,* "Techniques for the Diagnosis and Measurement of Intergroup Attitudes and Behavior," *Psychological Bulletin,* 45 (1948), 248-71.

tion of a program. When, for example, we know the total history of an attempt on the part of a trade union or industry to abolish discrimination, or we feel (though we cannot prove) that we know the cause and effect relations involved and how well the attempt succeeded.

(2) *Social barometer.* The increase or decrease of public discriminatory acts may be a useful guide. Complaints to the police, or incidents in street cars, restaurants, employment agencies—all may indicate the effects of current forces at work within .. community.

(3) *Content analysis of public records.* The number of discriminatory advertisements in newspapers, or the filing of legislative bills, or the nature of political speeches, usefully extend the conception of a social barometer.

(4) *Questionnaires and scales.* The most commonly employed device is the before-and-after test used with the same individuals, and, where possible, with a control group. The tests may be designed to measure knowledge, beliefs, or attitudes.

(5) *Public opinion polls.* Trends of favor or disfavor toward minority groups can be noted from poll interviews held in the same locality before and after a program is tried.

(6) *Changes in population and in community activities.* Minority groups may grow more separated or more intermingled as a result of programs. New intergroup projects may be inaugurated. Changes in the composition of community agencies may result.

(7) *Participation indices.* In certain cases the amount that behavior has changed may be gauged by noting the increased time that a person spends with members of minority groups or devotes to intergroup activities.

(8) *Sociometry.* Choices of playmates, friends, or teammates may alter following a program.

(9) *Projective and pictorial techniques.* Tests that avoid direct questioning are gaining in favor. The indi-

vidual may show a shift in his aggressive, affiliative, or rejective tendencies by reacting differently to pictures, to sentence completion tests, or in his telling of stories.

(10) *Miscellaneous other measures.* The above list is not exhaustive. One might include "reasoning tests" to see whether a given program has enhanced people's ability to think clearly. So with "perceptual" and "cognitive" tests to see whether people think less rigidly and perceive differences more adequately.

EDUCATIONAL CURRICULA

As Professor Cook has pointed out, modern educational methods in intergroup relations are becoming more resourceful and imaginative. At least six widely different types of teaching devices can be identified.[7] (1) There is the "informational approach," imparting knowledge by lectures and textbook teaching. (2) The "vicarious experience approach" employs movies, dramas, fiction, and other devices that invite the student to identify with members of an outgroup. (3) The "community study-action approach" calls for field trips, area surveys, work in social agencies or community programs. (4) "Exhibits, festivals and pageants" encourage a sympathetic regard for the customs of minority groups and our Old World heritage. (5) The "small group process" applies principles of group dynamics, including discussion, sociodrama, and group re-training. Finally, there is (6) the "individual conference" where therapeutic or advisory interviewing is employed.

We are not yet able to say categorically which of these six approaches brings the greatest return. In an unpublished study Mrs. Natalie Fuchs surveyed thirty-seven evaluative studies utilizing these various approaches singly or in combination. She finds that twenty-seven report positive results, and ten equivocal;

[7]Cook, *op. cit.*, p. 15.

scarcely any were negative. But of the twenty-seven having positive results only nine could be considered statistically significant. And only about one-quarter of the total number employed control groups.

While it is fairly certain that desirable effects appear in approximately two-thirds of the experiments, and ill effects very rarely, we still do not know for sure what methods are most successful. The trend of evidence as Cook points out, seems to favor *indirect* approaches. By indirect we mean programs that do not specialize in the study of minority groups as such, nor focus upon the phenomena of prejudice as such. The student seems to gain more when he loses himself in community projects, when he participates in realistic situations, and develops, as William James would say, "acquaintance with" the field rather than "knowledge about" the field.

This tentative conclusion clearly puts the *informational approach* on the defensive. And since education has traditionally, both in theory and practice, concerned itself primarily with the imparting of information, the issue demands close scrutiny.

It has always been thought that planting right ideas in the mind would engender right behavior. But with the decline of ideo-motor theory in psychology came the realization that ethical training, education for citizenship and character, require much more than the imparting of information. The student's readiness to learn facts, it is now pretty well agreed, depends upon the state of his attitudes. Information seldom sticks unless mixed with attitudinal glue. Facts themselves are inhuman; only attitudes are human. Thus it comes about that purely factual training often has one of three equally abortive results: it is soon forgotten; or it is distorted in such a way as to rationalize existing attitudes; or the information is allowed to sit in one corner of the mind isolated from the main determinants of living conduct.

This segregation of knowledge from conduct is revealed in the few investigations that have tested both beliefs and attitudes. Authoritative instruction does seem to have the power of correcting erroneous beliefs even if it fails appreciably to alter attitudes. Samelson's research is a case in point.[8] In a national sample she found that well-educated people were considerably more correct than less educated people in their factual statements regarding the Negro, but only slightly more favorable in their attitudes. Some years ago the effects of an educational tour of Japan for high school students was evaluated. The gain on an information test given before and after was enormous, but there was no significant change in attitudes toward the Japanese people.[9]

One reason for this disconcerting finding lies in the tendency of informational instruction to exaggerate the unity of the ethnic, national, or religious groups under study. Emphasis is mistakenly placed on the unique history or distinguishing marks of the group and on its inner cohesiveness and distinctive culture. While the student may thus gain a more accurate picture of the group, he is at the same time tempted to categorize it more firmly than ever; and if he happens not to like the group, the categorization abets rather than weakens his prejudice. The very essence of prejudice we know lies in the fallacious assumption that every member of a group, simply because he is a member, has the qualities that are presumed to apply to the group as a whole.

Yet there is an argument to be made on the opposite side. Perhaps students may in the short run show no gains or may

[8]B. Samelson, "Does Education Diminish Prejudice?" *Journal of Social Issues,* 1 (1945), 11-13.

[9]Cited in A. M. Rose, *Studies in Reduction of Prejudice* (Mimeographed, Chicago: American Council on Race Relations, 1947), p. 51.

twist the facts to serve their prejudices. But in the long run accurate information will have its impact. Truth, we must assume, is ultimately the ally of improved human relations. To take an example: Myrdal points out that there is no longer any intellectually respectable "race" theory that can justify the position of the Negro in this country. Since people are not wholly irrational, this fact is gradually penetrating their attitudes. Already it may be said to have weakened the stability of the caste system, even though its effects are as yet not fully evident.

Again, the fundamental premise of intercultural education says in effect, no person knows his own culture who knows only his own culture. A child who grows up to believe that the sun rises and sets on his own ingroup, and who views foreigners as strange beings from the outer darkness, is a child lacking perspective on the conditions of his own life. He will never see the American way for what it is—one of many alternative patterns of living that men have invented for their needs. Without intercultural information obtained at school a child cannot acquire this perspective, for most children come from homes and neighborhoods where they have no opportunity to learn about outgroups in an objective way. They learn about them only in terms of erroneous stereotypes saturated with derision or hostility. Of course, the school may fail to offset the home-made attitude, but it is certainly logical to suppose that an improvement in attitude cannot be achieved unless the child's muddled ideas are corrected.

But you ask, may not scientific and factual instruction contain information *unfavorable* to minority groups? Yes, it is conceivable that the incidence of evil traits may be higher in one group than in another. If so, this information should not be suppressed. If we are going after the truth we must go after the whole of it—not merely after the part that is congenial.

Enlightened members of minority groups do, I think, favor the publication of *all* scientific and factual findings; for they are convinced that when the whole truth is known it will show that most of the common stereotypes and accusations are false. If a small percentage of the accusations prove to be justified on the average, the proper explanation of the findings in terms of the adverse conditions under which many minority groups live will improve our perspective on the problem and motivate reform.

How shall we sum up? Information, we concede, does not necessarily alter either attitude or action. What is more, its gains, according to available research, seem slighter than those of other educational methods employed. At the same time there is virtually no evidence that sound factual information does any harm. Perhaps its value may be long delayed, and may consist in driving wedges of doubt and discomfort into the stereotypes of the prejudiced. It seems likely, too, that the greater gains ascribed to action and project methods require sound factual instruction as underpinning. All in all, we do well to resist the irrationalist position that invites us to abandon entirely the traditional ideals and methods of formal education. Facts may not be enough, but they still seem indispensable.

A related question arises concerning the merits of focusing attention directly upon intergroup problems. Is it well, for example, for children to discuss the "Negro problem," or is it better for them to learn facts through more incidental methods? Some people think that courses in English or geography supply a better context for intercultural studies than courses focused directly on social issues. Others argue that the really important influence is highly indirect—namely, the structure of the school system itself. Children who study in a segregated or authoritarian atmosphere will certainly not learn the lessons of democracy and tolerance.

Without debate we can concede the point that there is surely no reason to sharpen in the child's mind a sense of conflict. Far better for him to learn the similarities among human groups and to take for granted the fact that friendly adjustment is possible. Yet we cannot be categorical about the matter. For while a child may through indirect methods learn to take cultural pluralism for granted, he is still perplexed by visible differences in skin color, by the recurrent Jewish holidays, by religious diversity. His education is incomplete unless he understands these matters. Some degree of directness would seem to be required.

And with older and more sophisticated people there may be even greater value in a direct approach, particularly with advanced students who are prepared to face issues head-on. In an experiment devoted to three modes of teaching at one-week seminars Rabbi Kagan reports greatest gains by the direct method.[10] Students were of high school age and selected for their interest in religious matters. Most of them were thus probably prepared to face issues frankly and to shift their attitudes in a favorable direction. Similar consideration may account for some of the success found in intercultural workshops for teachers and social workers where direct methods are employed.

In respect to other educational methods, some evidence indicates that films, novels, dramas may be effective, presumably because they induce identification with minority group members. In one study of eighth-grade children this approach was found more effective than either the informational or the direct-participation approach.[11] If this finding stands up in repeated research we shall be confronted with an interesting

[10]H. E. Kagan, *Changing Attitudes of Christians Toward Jews* (New York: Columbia University Press, 1952).

[11]Cited in Cook, *op. cit.*, p. 34.

49

possibility. It may be that the strategies of realistic participation constitute too strong a threat to some people. A milder invitation to identification at the fantasy level may be a more effective first step. Perhaps in the future we shall decide that intercultural programs should start with fiction, drama and films, and move gradually into more realistic methods of training.

In spite of what has just been said, there seems to be widespread agreement among educators that for many students and adults the best techniques for reducing group tensions involve cooperative undertakings. For this reason efforts are made to get people of different cultures and classes to work together for common objectives, to participate as neighbors in matters of mutual concern, and to take part jointly and without sentimentality in recreational and community activities.

CONTACT AND ACQUAINTANCE METHODS

Contact brings friendliness. This assumption lies at the basis of many current action programs. It is, however, stated far too broadly. While some kinds of contact seem to make for mutual understanding and friendliness, the reverse is also true. Prejudice seems to be increased by casual, public contacts in urban situations, for such contacts serve to reinforce stereotypes and remind people of their rivalries. Likewise contact between members of groups having very different economic and social statuses lends constant reinforcement to the conviction of one group that it is inherently superior and justifies the resentments of the other. Nor are contacts helpful between members of two groups who equally lack status—for example, between poor whites and poor blacks, or between two impoverished immigrant groups, for each is intent upon establishing status at the expense of the other. Nor are residential contacts helpful if these are perceived by the established group in terms of a threatening invasion.

Yet studies are accumulating to show that under certain conditions increased contact makes for lessened prejudice. These studies are so much in agreement in their findings that we may venture to state a tentative law: *Prejudice tends to diminish whenever members of different groups meet on terms of equal status in the pursuit of common objectives.* Supporting evidence is drawn from several sources:

(1) White soldiers who have fought side by side with Negro troops in combat are much more favorable to Negroes than are white soldiers who have not had this experience.[12] The magnitude of the difference is so great that it probably cannot be accounted for by the special conditions that obtained at the time of the study, namely, that the Negroes were selected volunteers and that their officers were white.

(2) It has been found that white collar employees in a government office who had known Negroes on the job with status equal to their own were more favorably disposed than those who had not. Likewise, university students who had known professionally trained Negroes were less prejudiced than those who had not.

(3) Initial studies of public housing projects indicate that white people who live in integrated housing units with Negroes as close neighbors are more favorably disposed than those who live in segregated units. Nor does it seem that the initial selection of tenants is wholly responsible for this finding, although this particular question needs to be clarified in the course of future research.

12S. A. Stouffer, *et al., The American Soldier: Adjustment during Army Life.* Vol. I of "Studies in Social Psychology in World War II" (Princeton: University Press, 1949), Chap. 10.

(4) The research of F. Tredwell Smith belongs here.[13] Closer intellectual and social contact of college students with Negro life in Harlem resulted in gains in tolerance. While students had previously rubbed elbows in casual contact with many Negroes it required the approach of equal status and common interest to increase their friendliness. Similar results have been reported in relationships with Jews. Prejudice appears to be directly related to frequency of personal contact but inversely related to intimacy of personal contact. Allport and Kramer's findings are consistent with these conclusions.[14]

The law, it will be recalled, contains two propositions: first, that the contact must be one of equal status; and, second, that the members must have objective interests in common. While it may help to place members of groups side by side on a job, the gain in tolerance is greater if these members regard themselves as part of a team. Kurt Lewin has pointed out that many committees on race or community relations do not really engage in common projects of mutual interest. They merely meet to talk about the problem. Lacking a definite objective goal such goodwill committees often experience frustration and disillusionment.

The application of the law calls for strategy. For example, it has been argued that a personnel man may do well to start his nondiscrimination policy by employing minority group members in his own department, or at the top management level. Others have said that it is better to start the process in those departments where the threat to status is less noticeable. Whether or not it is better to poll the employees in advance is also a disputed question. Watson points out how in cities,

[13]F. T. Smith, *An Experiment in Modifying Attitudes Toward the Negro* (New York: Teachers College, Columbia University, 1943).

[14]G. W. Allport and B. M. Kramer, "Some Roots of Prejudice," *Journal of Psychology*, 22 (1946), 9-39.

like Cleveland, Negroes have taken their place as drivers and conductors on street cars and busses.[15] The change soon ceased to attract attention. In Philadelphia, however, the mere proposal to hire Negro operators precipitated a crippling strike, although six months later Negro drivers were taken for granted and a Negro was elected to union office.

All considerations point the sure moral that artificial segregation should be abolished. Until it is abolished equal status contacts cannot take place, thus cooperative projects of joint concern cannot arise. And until this condition is fulfilled we may not expect widespread resolution of intergroup tensions. Hence nearly all investigators agree that *the attack on segregation must continue.* Gandhi, it will be remembered, called for the elimination of untouchability as the first point in his program of non-violent reform.

One final word of caution concerning the law. It would be easy to point to apparent exceptions. But usually these exceptions are not actual test cases. For example, it has been found that boys in a mixed school were as prejudiced against Negroes as were boys in an all-white school. Apparently equal-status contact did not have the expected result. But status is a subtle thing—and minority groups in a school system do not always enjoy equality. Furthermore, as we have seen, contact alone is not enough. The contact must lead to common action in the pursuit of common ends. In many schools this form of mutuality does not occur. Last but not least, this law, like all social laws, can claim to hold only when other things are equal. It is quite possible that counter-currents may set the law temporarily in abeyance. But the existence of such countertides does not mean that there are no lawful currents in human relations.

[15]Goodwin Watson, *Action for Unity* (New York: Harper and Brothers, 1947), p. 63.

GROUP RETRAINING

It is a widely held dogma in social science that it is easier to change the attitudes of a whole group of people than to change the attitudes of one person within the group. Whether this dogma yet deserves the status of a scientific law is hard to say. There is some impressive evidence in its favor. Research on group decision is pertinent. When members in concert vote to try an innovation, whether in matters of family diet or in attaining a new level of production on the job the results seem better than those achieved by any other method tried in connection with the same experiment. Lippitt reports that members trained in community relations work were more active in carrying through their projects when others trained at the same time were likewise active in the community.[16] Workers who became isolated in regions where no other members of the training team lived seemed less effective. Their attitudes had no social support. To broaden the ground for the generalization, we note that alcoholics control their addiction best when they are members of a group of fellow sufferers.

One of the boldest advances in modern social science is the deliberate formation of groups for the express purpose of recentering their attitudes and habits. Assuming that such a group of willing subjects can be found, it starts its work with one great psychological advantage. Whether the subject knows it in advance or not his total personality will soon be involved. Unlike the citizen who reads a pamphlet or listens to a sermon on brotherhood, the individual who submits himself to a retraining program is in it up to his eyes. He is involved through discussion, role playing, and the exposure of his own weaknesses. He is brought up short by the feedback technique whereby his failure to make progress is revealed to him. Time

[16]Ronald Lippitt, *Training in Community Relations* (New York: Harper and Brothers, 1949).

and again his complacency is shocked, and the shock is continued until he alters his ways. While this painful process continues, he finds he is growing more and more identified with the research itself, and more and more anxious for beneficial changes to occur. And when changes do occur they are likely to be deep and effective for they have taken place not in segmental regions of the mind but in the whole person.

Now there are two principal styles of retraining. One is of the direct order just described. It calls for a considerable amount of self-criticism and self-consciousness. In this respect it is like deliberate therapy. Indeed, leaders in this field report that individual therapeutic conferences are a desirable supplement.

The other type is more objectively centered. The retraining is a by-product of outward accomplishment. An example of this type is the community self-survey. Volunteers band together to study their region. This step is the diagnostic phase—and leads primarily to knowledge concerning common problems. Along the way participants develop skills in working together. The second stage comes when it is clear that additional skills need to be developed and new social policies inaugurated in order to improve the situation found to exist.

Another example of outwardly centered retraining is found in connection with the technique known as incident control. Its purpose, as in any group retraining, is to break down inhibition and rigidity in several individuals at once, so that they may become more effective in the pursuit of common ends. In this case, those who submit to training wish to develop a skill for use in every-day life—skill in offsetting the bigoted remarks that stain our national habits of conversation. What does one say, for example, to a stranger in a public place who has made a venomous comment on the Jews? Of course there are many situations where propriety says, "Keep silent," but there are other situations where silence would lend consent and where our sense of justice prompts us to speak up. Research shows that a calm tone of voice, marked by obvious sincerity, and expressing the view that such comments are un-American, has the most favorable effect on bystanders. But it is not easy to summon courage to speak at all, let alone find the right words and control one's voice. Hours of practice under supervision in a group setting are required. It is along these lines that Citron, Chein and Harding have been working.[17]

All of the retraining programs discussed thus far have one limitation. They are designed to free the tolerant person of his inhibitions and to provide him with skills if he wants them. It is clear that full-scale group retraining cannot be used with people who resist both the method and its objectives. Yet it is not inconceivable that with patience and tact groups or classes formed for other purposes may be led by easy stages into practicing the techniques of group dynamics. Before this point is reached, it may be necessary to allow members of the group to unburden themselves of pent-up hostile feelings. Such catharsis will often prepare the way for constructive training.

Furthermore, partial use of the techniques of group dynamics may be made without going the whole way. School children, for example, may easily be led into role playing. By playing the part of a child in an outgroup the juvenile actor may learn through his own organic sensations something of the suffering and defensiveness engendered by discrimination.

MASS MEDIA

There are good grounds for doubting the effectiveness of mass propaganda. People whose ears and eyes are bombarded

17A. F. Citron, *et al.*, "Anti-Minority Remarks: A Problem for Action Research," *Journal of Abnormal and Social Psychology*, 45 (1950), 99-126.

all day with the blandishments of special interests tend to develop a propaganda blindness and deafness. And what chance has a mild message of brotherhood when sandwiched in between layers of war, intrigue, hatred and crime? What is more, pro-tolerance propaganda is selectively perceived. Those who do not want to admit it to their sanctuaries of belief find no trouble in evading it. Uusually those who admit it do not need it. Other people contrive to reverse or distort the message to suit their own prejudgments.

But this general pessimism should not block our search for more detailed knowledge. After all, we know that advertising and films have molded our national culture to a considerable degree. May they not profiably be used in the task of remolding it?

Research, though still somewhat meagre, suggests even now certain tentative laws:

(1) While single programs—a film perhaps—show slight effects, several related programs produce effects apparently even greater than could be accounted for in terms of simple summation. This principle of pyramiding stimulation is well understood by practical propagandists. Any publicity expert knows that a single program is not enough; there must be a campaign.

(2) A second tentative principle concerns the specificity of effect. Let me illustrate. In the spring of 1951 a motion picture theater in Boston ran the film *The Sound of Fury*. The picture concluded with the clearly stated moral that conflicts can be solved only through patience and understanding, not through violence. The audience, deeply moved by the dramatic story, applauded the moral. Later in the same program a news reel depicted Senator Taft speaking on international relations. He made the identical point that conflict can be solved only through patience and understanding, not through violence. The

same audience hissed. What they had learned in one context did not carry over to another. Recent researches confirm the point of little transfer of training.[18]

(3) A third principle has to do with attitude regression. After a period of time opinions tend to slip back toward the original point of view, but not all the way.

(4) This regression, however, is not universal. Studying both the short-run and the long-run effect of indoctrination films in the Army, Hovland and others found that while attitude regression was common enough, in some people a reverse trend occurred. "Sleeper effects" came to light in die-hards who at first resist the message of the film but later accept it. These delayed responses are noted especially among well-educated people whose initial opinions are contrary to those held by most other educated people. The authors suggest that latently these individuals have predispositions favoring the propaganda message but first overcome some inner resistance to it. The moral seems to be that pro-tolerance propaganda reaching people who are ambivalent in their attitudes may have long-range effects, especially among the better educated portions of the population.

(5) Propaganda is more effective when there are no deep-seated resistances. The research of Bettelheim and Janowitz shows that people who are "on the fence" are more likely to be affected than those who are deeply committed.[19]

(6) Propaganda is more effective when it has a clear field. The monopoly of propaganda that exists in totalitarian lands forces a monotonous barrage upon the defenseless citizen, and he cannot long maintain his power of resistance. Counter-

18For example, C. I. Hovland, et al., *Experiments in Mass Communication*, Vol III of "Studies in Social Psychology in World War II (Princeton: University Press, 1949).

19B. Bettelheim and M. Janowitz, "Reactions to Fascist Propaganda: A Pilot Study," *Public Opinion Quarterly*, 14 (1950), 53-60.

propaganda, if it is permitted, throws the individual back upon his own resources of judgment, and frees him from a one-sided view of reality. In the light of this principle it may well be argued that pro-tolerance propaganda is needed—not so much for its positive effects but as an antidote to agitators who work on the other side.

(7) To be effective, propaganda should allay anxiety. Bettelheim and Janowitz found that propaganda striking at the roots of a person's frame of security tends to be resisted. Appeals geared into existing systems of security were more effective.

(8) A final principle concerns the importance of prestigeful symbols. A Kate Smith can sell millions of dollars in war bonds over the radio in a single day. An Eleanor Roosevelt, a Bing Crosby, have prestige for great masses of people. Their espousing of tolerance may win many fence straddlers, even though they cause people with die-hard prejudice to scream with resentment.

LEGISLATION

The past decade has seen far more anti-discrimination laws written into the statutes of our states than has any other period in history. During nine months of 1949, for example, 149 bills opposing discrimination were introduced into state legislatures. While only a small number of these bills were passed, there has been a steady accumulation of laws barring group libel and forbidding discrimination in employment, in education, in public housing, and elsewhere. Moving at a slower pace, but still moving, are legislative repeals of alien land acts, of mandatory segregation in education, of poll tax requirements for voting, of restrictive covenants. All national political parties officially favor a strong program of federal civil rights legislation, though the movement is for the present blocked by filibuster. At the same time all recent Supreme Court rulings in this area have insisted that the Constitution is color-blind, and that anti-discrimination laws are in principle valid.

The task of evaluating legislation seems to be beyond the capacity of present-day social science. Only the coarsest of measures can be used. Thus in 1950 *Business Week* sent an inquiry to several large employers in states having a statutory Fair Employment Practices Commission, asking in effect, "Does the State FEPC hamper you?" The editors summarize the opinions by saying, "FEPC laws haven't caused near the fuss that opponents predicted. Disgruntled job seekers haven't swamped commissions with complaints. Personal friction hasn't been at all serious. . . . Even those who opposed an FEPC aren't actively hostile now." Furthermore, employers seem agreed that the law has not interfered with their "basic right to select the most competent workers."[20]

This evaluation, so far as it goes, deals only with the negative aspect of the legislation, proving merely that no great harm has resulted. On the positive side we have testimonies from several FEPC states that hundreds of complaints are settled through amicable adjustment. One undoubted result is that many employers open their industries and businesses for the first time to members of minority groups. Rarely is it necessary to take a case to court.

Other types of legislation are still more difficult to evaluate. The best we can do at present is to offer a psychological guess concerning the conditions under which legislation is effective. The guess states that people *will accept and generally obey laws that support what their consciences tell them is right.* So deep in our conscience lies the American Creed that we tend to welcome laws to implement its realization. Now, of

[20]*Business Week,* February 25, 1950, pp. 114-17.

course, all laws are dishonored in the breach. People approve traffic laws, but often violate them; they certainly approve laws against rape; yet rapes occur. There are always in society some individuals so compulsive that laws will not deter them from anti-social acts. There are also mores and local vested interests so entrenched that they are able to prevent the passage of anti-discriminatory legislation, or to nullify it if enacted.

In the United States there are obviously regional differences in the above respects. But throughout most of the states there is only a minority of individuals so fatally fixed in their ethnic attitudes that they cannot be influenced by the changing social climate that legislation helps to create. These individuals —Merton calls them "all weather illiberals"—correspond to our inveterate traffic violators and tax dodgers. Laws don't change them. Laws merely make it clear that their behavior is judged inimical to the public welfare and is in violation of public policy. The argument for anti-discrimination legislation (assuming, of course, that it is technically sound) is that it has the power to define the norms for acceptable conduct. Legislation is never aimed directly at the reduction of prejudice. Rather it establishes conditions of psychological and social equality of status, under which, we know from other research, prejudice tends to diminish.

INDIVIDUAL THERAPY

In theory, we should expect to find the maximum amount of change in attitudes under conditions of individual psychotherapy. The person in distress who seeks the aid of a psychiatrist or counselor is usually at the end of his tether. His attitudes are potentially in a fluid state. Whether he knows it or not, and whether he wishes it or not, he is ripe for a realignment of many of his basic orientations toward life. Even his ethnic prejudices, if they come to light at all during the therapy, are likely to be shaken up and perhaps dissolved along with his other fixed ways of looking at life.

It is true, Dr. Simmel has remarked, that no patient approaches a therapist primarily to be cured of a prejudice. Like most of us, the patient has his biases well rationalized and deeply embedded. Yet it not infrequently happens—especially in the course of psychoanalytic therapy—that these biases assume a salient role. Indeed, in principle, we should expect that whenever prejudice of any sort intersects a neurosis, the cure of the neurosis should result in a reduction of the prejudice. While this matter has been discussed by various writers from the psychoanalytic point of view, there are as yet no statistics concerning the extent of such cures.

Nor is psychoanalysis the only therapeutic technique that should result in transformations. Any individual with a potentiality for fair-mindedness is likely to re-assess many of his attitudes in the course of therapy. In fact such re-assessment may take place even in a series of interviews not primarily therapeutic in intent. On one occasion, students working under my supervision conducted interviews, often several hours in length, with ordinary citizens who agreed to tell about their attitudes toward minority groups. It not infrequently happened that the series began with expressions of marked hostility, and ended with manifestly lessened prejudice. One woman talked for several hours about her attitude toward Jews. Bitter at the start, her comments became more and more objective. Gradually catharsis gave way to self-criticism. At the conclusion of the sessions she had gained some insight into the role of anti-Semitism in her own personality, and summarized her final position in the words, "The poor Jews. I guess we blame them for everything, don't we?"

The frequency of such transformations under therapeutic or quasi-therapeutic interviewing is unknown. Much more research in this area is needed. But even if this method proves to be the most effective of all methods—as on a priori grounds it should be—the proportion of the population reached will always be small.

THE STRUCTURAL ARGUMENT, CRITIQUE

Our survey leaves us with some perplexing questions. Why, for example, is information apparently of slight value in changing behavior? Why do attitudes tend to regress following an initial change? Why is the effect of propaganda specific rather than generalized? Why do tolerant attitudes expressed in words so often fail to find their way into tolerant conduct? Why, in short, do programs of action have somewhat meagre effects? In spite of immense efforts in recent years we cannot say that intergroup relations have improved markedly.

The sociologist has an answer. He points out that all of us are trapped in one or more social systems. While these systems have some variability, they are not infinitely plastic. Furthermore, each system engenders certain inevitable tensions whenever there is inadequate housing, economic rivalry, crowded transportation facilities, or other frustrations inherent in the system. To meet the strain, tradition accords certain groups a superior, and other groups an inferior, position. Custom regulates the distribution of limited privileges, goods, and prestige. Any great increase in density or pressure from groups in inferior positions inevitably threatens the mode of life of the superior groups. Vested interests of various sorts are pivots within the system, and these in particular resist any attempts at basic change. Further, tradition earmarks certain groups as legitimate scapegoats within the system. Hostility is taken for granted. Hoodlums are tolerated as by-products of the existing strain. Even chiefs of police may wink at ethnic gang fights. They are normal and natural "kid stuff." To be sure, if the disruption goes too far the riot squad is called out, or reformers press for legislative relief of the excess tension. But this relief is only sufficient to restore the uneasy equilibrium. If relief went too far it also would destroy the system.

While you and I are not normally aware of the extent to which our behavior is conditioned by the social system, we are nonetheless profoundly constrained by it. How can we expect a few detached hours of intercultural education to counteract in the child the total press of the social structure? In some localities intolerable ostracism or ridicule would fall upon the adolescent if he were friendly with Mexicans, Japanese, or Jews. A pro-Negro film in the South is automatically rejected as a threat to the foundations of the system. The theory holds that one cannot change segregation, employment customs, or immigration without letting off a chain of effects that would cumulate to produce threatening changes in the total structure. Each folkway is an ally of every other. If too strong an initial push is allowed it might lead to an acceleration of forces that would destroy the whole system, and therewith our sense of security. Such is the structural view of the sociologist.

The psychologist, too, has a structural argument. A prejudiced attitude is not like a cinder in the eye that can be extracted without disturbing the integrity of the organism as a whole. On the contrary, prejudice is often so deeply embedded in character-structure that it cannot be changed unless the entire inner economy of the life is overhauled. Such embeddedness occurs whenever attitudes have functional significance for the organism. It has been shown, for example, that a person's attitude toward Russia is often a mere reflection of his whole philosophy of life. The same rule applies to the central place of prejudice in the "authoritarian personality." You cannot expect to change the part without changing the whole, and it is never easy to remake the whole of a personality.

But the psychologist hastens to add that not all attitudes are deeply embedded. A three-fold distinction seems helpful.

(1) There is first the individual who keeps his attitudes closely in touch with his own first-hand experience while making allowance for social custom and demand. He manages to adjust attitudes to social reality with little friction while remaining entirely true to his own store of experience.

For this type we might expect attitudes to change as information concerning social reality is acquired. Thus he is open to information concerning minority groups, and such information may change his opinions. He sees clearly that the existing social system makes it hard for minority groups. He therefore favors remedial legislation, and in general gears his attitudes to rational considerations.

(2) The second class of attitudes, however, are those we have spoken of. They form an internal integration that is self-serving, rigid, often neurotic. Realism is low. The individual neither knows nor cares what the facts are concerning minority groups, nor how harmful in the long run are the discriminatory customs that prevail. The functional significance of these attitudes lies deep, and nothing short of an upheaval in the character-structure will change them.

(3) Finally, and frequently, we find that the ethnic attitudes of many individuals lack internal integration. They are shifting and amorphous, and for the most part linked to the situation. The person himself may be said to be ambivalent, or, more accurately, multi-valent, for, lacking a firm attitude structure, he bends with every pressure. It is with this group that "irrational" appeals may be most effective. Pleasant experiences, dramatic lessons, invocations of the American Creed, may be sufficient to provide for the incipient crystallization of a friendly attitude. This type is particularly susceptible to propaganda and to rewarding experience that will start a definite mental set

where before there has been only opportunistic conformity to prevailing prejudice.

We have no way of knowing how numerous each of these types may be. The strictly structural point of view would insist that all of them are affected more than we know by the personal and social systems in which they are set.

Some authors stress the interlocking dependence of both the personal and the social system. Thus, Vallance argues that one must attack an attitude with due regard to both kinds of systems which in combination hold the attitude embedded in a structural matrix.[21] And Newcomb states that "attitudes tend to be persistent (relatively unchanging) when the individual continues to perceive objects in a more or less stable frame of reference."[22] Now a stable frame of reference may be anchored in the social environment. (All immigrants live on one side of the tracks, all native Americans on the other.) Or it may be an inner frame of reference. (I am threatened by these immigrants). Or it may be both. This combined structural view would insist that a shift in all relevant frames of reference must precede change in attitude.

Whether sociological, psychological, or both, the structural point of view has merit. It explains why piecemeal efforts are not more effective than they are. It tells us that our problem is lockstitched into our social personalities. It convinces us that the cinder-in-the-eye theory of social attitudes is too simple.

Yet, if we are not careful, the structural view may lead both to false psychology and to false pessimism. It really is not sensible to say that before we change personal attitudes we must change total structure; for in part at least the structure

[21]T. R. Vallance, "Methodology in Propaganda Research," *Psychological Bulletin,* 48 (1951), 32-61.

[22]T. M. Newcomb, *Social Psychology* (New York: Dryden Press, 1950), p. 233.

is the product of the attitudes of many single people. **Change must begin somewhere.** Indeed according to the structural theory it may start anywhere, for every system is to some extent altered by the change in any of its parts. A social or a psychological system is an equilibrium of forces, but it is an unstable equilibrium. The "American dilemma," for example, as Myrdal shows, results from such instability. All our official definitions of the social system call for equality, while many (not all) of the informal features of this system call for inequality. There is thus a state of "unstructuredness" in even our most structured systems. And while your personality or mine is certainly a system, can we say that it is impervious to change, or that alteration in the whole must precede alteration of parts? Such a view would be obscurantist.

CONCLUSIONS

It is, therefore, perfectly sensible to ask, Where shall change begin? What parts of the system may we attack in order to bring about final alteration in the whole? The present paper has sought to summarize our knowledge in this area as of the present time. Some of our principal conclusions are the following:

(1) Since the problem is manysided there is no sovereign formula, nor any single method so effective that it commands our primary allegiance. The wisest thing to do is to attack all fronts simultaneously. If no single attack has large effect, yet many small attacks from many directions can have large cumulative effects.

(2) Meliorism must be our guide. People who talk in terms of the ultimate assimilation of all minority groups into one ethnic stock are speaking of a distant Utopia. To be sure, there would be no minority group problems in a homogeneous society, but it seems probable that in this country at least our

loss through homogeneity would be greater than our gain. In any case, it is certain that artificial attempts to hasten assimilation will not succeed. We shall improve human relations only by learning to live with racial and cultural pluralism for a long time to come.

(3) It is reasonable to expect that our efforts will have some upsetting effects. The attack on a system always has. Thus a person who has been exposed to intercultural education, to tolerance propaganda, to role playing, may show greater inconsistency of behavior than before. But from the point of view of attitude change this state of "unstructuredness" is a necessary stage. A wedge has been driven that may never be withdrawn. While the individual may be more uncomfortable than before, he has at least a chance of recentering his outlook in a more tolerant manner. Investigation shows that people who are aware of, and ashamed of, their prejudices are well on the road to eliminating them.

(4) Occasionally there may be a boomerang effect. Efforts may serve only to stiffen opposition in defense of existing attitudes or offer people unintended support for their hostile opinions. Such evidence as we have indicates that this result is relatively slight. It is also a question whether the effect may not be temporary, for any strategy effective enough to arouse defensiveness is likely to be strong enough to plant seeds of misgiving. It seems probable, too, that boomerangs occur chiefly in minds with paranoid trends where any stimulus is absorbed into a rigid system. To be sure, there is the ever present danger that a given program may be so badly presented that the public cannot understand its intended meaning. But boomerangs in this sense are due merely to ineptitude and to the failure to pre-test the program, and thus are avoidable.

(5) From what we know of mass media, it seems wise not to expect marked results from this method alone. Rela-

tively few people are in the precise stage of "unstructuredness," and in precisely the right frame of mind, to admit the message. Further, it seems well, on the basis of existing evidence, to focus mass propaganda on specific issues, such for example as FEPC rather than upon vague appeals. Whether advertising the message of brotherhood is effective, we simply do not know. Research in this area is needed.

(6) It seems probable that greatest value comes from programs that incite deep first-hand experiences. A person's pre-existing pride or his pre-existing circles of affection and affiliation may lead him to resist influences that challenge these ego-involved motives, unless these motives themselves are effectively engaged.

(7) For this reason the teacher or group leader will offer information and new experience within a framework that will allow the individual to maintain his system of pride and affection even while he learns to enlarge it. By working in the community, for example, he may learn that neither his self-esteem nor his attachments are threatened by Negro neighbors. He can even learn that his own security and self-respect are strengthened when social conditions in his town are improved. He can understand that the United Nations, our "last and best hope for peace," will succeed only if the white nations of the earth cease their condescension toward colored nations and colored minorities. In short, for permanent, long-run results, we must be led to see that we have much to gain in terms of security and happiness by inviting more people into our circle.

(8) From this point of view, it is not apology or special pleading for this or that minority group that is needed. What is needed is emphasis upon national and international solidarity, community welfare, and common moral codes. While preaching and exhortation may play their part in the process, the lesson

will not be learned at the verbal level alone. It will be learned in muscle, nerve, and gland by child and adult only when it is worked out through participant citizenship.

(9) Hence we see why educators insist upon a democratic school structure to begin with and favor project methods in intercultural education rather than informational methods. Evidence, so far as it goes, supports their preference. Some slight indications also suggest that a good vestibule leading to more whole-hearted participation is the strategy of vicarious experience. Films and fiction may prepare the individual for the more virile lessons of community survey, role playing, and group dynamics.

(10) Since the very essence of prejudice is fallacious categorization concerning the alleged attributes of groups as a whole, prejudice will tend to disappear as children and adults are encouraged to view others as individuals and to evaluate members of outgroups as separate persons. Unless people actually mingle with outgroups—that is, unless segregation is destroyed—they are not likely to learn this basic lesson of individualization.

(11) None of our commonly used methods is likely to work with bigots whose character-structure is so inaccessible that it demands the exclusion of outgroups as a condition of life. Yet strategies that will surely fail in some cases are not thereby damned, for they will not fail in all. Even for the rigid person there is left the possibility of individual therapy— an expensive method and one that is sure to be resisted; but in principle at least, we need not yet despair completely of the extreme case, especially if tackled young.

(12) Turning now to social programs, there is first of all widespread agreement that it is wiser to attack segregation and discrimination than to attack prejudice directly. For even if one dents the attitudes of the individual in isolation he is

still confronted by social barriers that he cannot surmount. And until segregation is weakened, conditions will not exist that permit equal status contacts in pursuit of common objectives.

(13) It would seem intelligent to take advantage of the vulnerable points where social change is most likely to occur. It has been pointed out that gains in housing and economic opportunities are on the whole the easiest to achieve. Fortunately it is these gains that minorities most urgently desire. Alert efforts along this line opened more than a million and a half jobs during World War II to workers previously excluded on the grounds of race and creed. Generally speaking, technological conditions in this country are fluid, and new opportunities continually occur. Admittedly it requires ingenuity to take advantage of them. But the general principle of pressing for housing reform and fair employment practices seems psychologically and socially sound.

(14) Generally speaking, a *fait accompli* that fits in with our democratic creed is accepted with little more than an initial flurry of protest. Cities that introduce Negroes into public jobs find that the change soon ceases to attract attention. Sound legislation and ordinance are similarly accepted. As MacIver has pointed out, official policies once established are hard to revoke. They set models that, once accepted, create habits and conditions favorable to their maintenance.

(15) While policy changes and legislation ordinarily mark painless advance, we cannot deny that strong and vociferous pressure may be needed before this gain is achieved. The organized demands of minority groups backed up by crusading and militant liberals have certainly been a factor in many of the gains thus far made. While such strife and contention do not in themselves resolve intergroup tensions, they may in the long run be the most effective factor in changing those parts

of the social system that need to be changed before solid gains can be made.

(16) The great peril resident in all ' ese programs is that, in our preoccupation with them, we fall into the totalitarian trap of manipulating people ·ith a handful of psychological tricks. Ultimately, there is no solution to intergroup tensions excepting through the inner growth of serene and benevolent persons who seek their own security and integrity not at the expense of their fellowmen, but in concert with them.

CHAPTER 4

Achieving Change in People, The Group Dynamics Approach

DORWIN CARTWRIGHT

*Director of Research Center for Group
Dynamics, University of Michigan.*

DORWIN CARTWRIGHT

Achieving Change in People,
The Group Dynamics Approach

Iᴛ ᴍᴀʏ ʙᴇ ᴡᴇʟʟ if we begin our discussion by facing directly the fact that the word *change* has emotional overtones. To many people it is threatening; it conjures up visions of a revolutionary, a dissatisfied idealist, a troublemaker, a malcontent. Nicer words referring to the process of changing people are *education, training, orientation, guidance, indoctrination,* and *therapy.* We are more ready to have others "educate" us than to have them "change" us. We, ourselves, feel less guilty in "training" others than in "changing" them.

Why an emotional response to these words? What makes the two kinds of terms have such different meanings? Part of the reason lies in the fact that the safer words (like *education* or *therapy*) carry the implicit assurance that the only changes produced will be good ones, acceptable within a presently held value system. The cold, unmodified word *change,* on the contrary, promises no respect for values; it might even tamper with values. Perhaps for this very reason it will foster straight thinking if we use the word *change* and thus force ourselves to struggle directly, self-consciously, with the problems of value

75

that are involved. Words like *education, training,* or *therapy* by the very fact that they are not so disturbing may close our eyes to the fact that they, too, inevitably involve values.

Another advantage of using the word *change* rather than other related words is that it leaves open the question of what aspects of people we are going to try to alter. Anyone familiar with the history of education knows that there has been endless controversy over what it is about people that education properly attempts to modify. Some educators have viewed education simply as imparting knowledge, others mainly as providing skills for doing things, still others as producing healthy "attitudes," and some have aspired to instill a way of life. Or if we choose to use a word like *therapy,* it can hardly be claimed that the term refers to a more clearly defined realm of change. Moreover, one can become inextricably entangled in distinctions and vested interests by attempting to distinguish sharply between, let us say, the domain of education and that of therapy. If we are to try to take a broader view and to develop some basic principles that promise to apply to all types of modifications in people, we had better use the word *change* to keep our thinking general enough.

GROUP DYNAMICS

One approach to change problems which is receiving considerable attention is that of group dynamics. What is this approach? What is meant by group dynamics? The word *dynamics* comes from a Greek term meaning force, and group dynamics refers to the forces operating in groups. The investigation of group dynamics, then, consists of a study of these forces: what gives rise to them, what conditions modify them, what consequences they have, etc. The practical application of group dynamics (or the technology of group dynamics) consists of the utilization of knowledge about these forces for the achievement of some purpose. So defined, group dynamics is not particularly novel, nor is it the exclusive property of any person or institution. Significant contributions to it have been made by such men as Simmel, Freud, and Cooley.

Although interest in groups has a long and respectable history, the past fifteen years have witnessed a new flowering of activity in this field. Today, research centers in several countries are carrying out substantial programs of study designed to reveal the nature of groups and their functioning. The field is being developed both as a branch of social science and as a form of social technology.

In this development the name of Kurt Lewin has been outstanding. As a consequence of his work, he became convinced of society's urgent need for a scientific approach to the understanding of the dynamics of groups. He devoted himself to meeting this need and in 1945 established the Research Center for Group Dynamics. The Center has been devoting its efforts to improving the scientific understanding of groups through laboratory experimentation, field studies, and the use of "action research." It has also attempted to help get the findings of social science more widely used by social management. Much of what I shall say is drawn from the experiences of the Center in its brief existence of a little more than six years.

CHANGE PROBLEMS, SOME EXAMPLES

For various reasons we have found that much of our work has been devoted to an attempt to gain a better understanding of the ways in which people change their behavior or resist efforts by others to have them do so. Whether we set for ourselves the practical goal of improving behavior or whether we take on the intellectual task of understanding why people do what they do, we have to investigate processes of communication, influence, social pressure—in short, problems of change.

In this work we have encountered great frustration. The issues have been most difficult to solve. Looking back over our experience I have become convinced that no small part of the trouble has resulted from an irresistible tendency to conceive of our problems in terms of the individual. We live in an individualistic culture. We value the individual highly, and rightly so. But I am inclined to believe that our political and social concern for the individual has narrowed our thinking as social scientists so much that we have not been able to state our research problems properly. Perhaps we have taken the individual as the unit of observation and study when some larger unit would have been more appropriate. Let us look at a few examples.

Consider first some matters having to do with the mental health of the individual. We can all agree, I believe, that an important mark of a healthy personality is that the individual's self-esteem has not been undermined. But on what does self-esteem depend? From research on this problem we have discovered that, among other things, repeated experiences of failure or traumatic failures on matters of central importance serve to undermine self-esteem. We also know that whether a person experiences success or failure as a result of some undertaking depends upon the level of aspiration which he has set for himself. Now, if we try to discover how the level of aspiration gets set, we are immediately involved in the person's relationships to groups. The groups to which he belongs set standards for his behavior which he must accept if he is to remain in the group. If his capacities do not allow him to reach these standards, he experiences failure. He withdraws or is rejected by the group and his self-esteem suffers a shock.

Suppose, then, that we accept the task of therapy, of rebuilding self-esteem. It would appear plausible that we should attempt to work with the sort of variables that produced the difficulty, that is, to work with an individual either in the groups to which he now belongs or to introduce him into new groups which are selected for the purpose, and then to concentrate on his relationships to groups as such. From the point of view of preventive mental health, we might even attempt to train the groups in our communities—classes in schools, work groups in business, families, unions, religious and cultural groups—to make use of practices better designed to protect the self-esteem of their members.

Consider a second example. A teacher finds that in her class she has a number of trouble-makers, full of aggression. She wants to know why these children are so aggressive and what can be done about it. A foreman in a factory has the same kind of problem with some of his workers. He wants the same kind of help. The solution most tempting to both the teacher and the foreman often is to transfer the worst trouble-makers to someone else, or, if facilities are available, to refer them for counseling. But is the problem really of such a nature that it can be solved by removing trouble-makers from the situation or by working on their individual motivations and emotional life?

Evidence on this problem indicates, of course, that there are many causes of aggressiveness, but the group aspect of the problem has become increasingly clear. If we observe carefully the amount of aggressive behaviors found in a large collection of groups, these behaviors will be seen to vary tremendously from group to group even when the different groups are composed of essentially the same kinds of people. In the now classic experiments of Lewin, Lippitt, and White[1] on the effects

[1] K. Lewin, R. Lippitt, and R. K. White, "Patterns of Aggressive Behavior in Experimentally Created 'Social Climates,'" *Journal of Social Psychology*, 10 (1939), 271-299.

of different styles of leadership, it was found that the same group of children displayed markedly different levels of aggressive behavior under different styles of leadership. Moreover, when individual children were transferred from one group to another, their levels of aggressiveness shifted to conform to the atmosphere of the new group. Efforts to account for child behaviors under any style of leadership merely in terms of personality traits could hardly succeed. This is not to say that a person's behavior is to be entirely accounted for by the atmosphere and structure of his immediate group, but it is remarkable to what an extent a strong, cohesive group can control aspects of a member's behavior which have been thought to be expressive of enduring personality traits. Recognition of this fact rephrases the problem of how to change human behavior. It directs us to a study of the sources of the influence of the group on its members.

Let us take an example from a different field. What can we learn from efforts to change people by mass media and mass persuasion? In those rare instances when educators, propagandists, advertisers, and others have made an objective evaluation of the enduring changes produced by their efforts, they have been able to demonstrate only the most negligible effects.[2] The inefficiency of attempts to influence the public by mass media would be scandalous if there were agreement that it was important or even desirable to have such influences be strongly exerted. In fact, it is no exaggeration to say that all of the research and experience of generations has not improved the efficiency of lectures or other means of mass influence to any noticeable degree. Something must be wrong with our theories of learning, motivation, and social psychology.

[2]Dorwin Cartwright, "Some Principles of Mass Persuasion: Selected Findings of Research on the Sale of United States War Bonds," *Human Relations,* 2 (1949), 253-267.

Within recent years, research data have been accumulating which may give us a clue to the solution of this problem. In one series of experiments directed by Lewin, it was found that a method of "group decision" in which the group as a whole makes a decision to have its members change their behavior was from two to ten times as effective in producing actual change as was a lecture presenting exhortation to change.[3] We have yet to learn precisely what produces these differences of effectiveness, but it is clear that by introducing group forces into the situation a whole new level of influence has been achieved.

The experience has been essentially the same when people have attempted to increase the productivity of individuals in work settings. Traditional conceptions of how to increase the output of workers have stressed the individual. Select the right man for the job; simplify the job for him; train him in the skills required; motivate him by economic incentives; make it clear to whom he reports; keep the lines of authority and responsibility simple and straight. But when all these conditions are fully met, we find that productivity is far below full potential. There is even good reason to conclude that this individualistic approach to productivity actually fosters negative consequences. The individual, isolated and subjected to the demands of the organization through the commands of his boss, finds that he must create with his fellow employees informal groups, not shown on any table of organization. Men do this to protect themselves from arbitrary control of their life, from the boredom produced by the endless repetition of mechanically sanitary and routine operations, and from the impoverishment of their emotional and social being which is brought about by the frustration of basic needs for social interaction, participa-

[3]Kurt Lewin, *Field Theory of Social Science* (New York: Harper and Brothers, 1951), pp. 229-236.

tion, and acceptance in groups. Recent experiments have demonstrated that work output can be greatly increased by methods of organization and supervision which give more responsibility to work groups, allow for fuller participation in important decisions, and make stable groups the firm basis for support of the individual's social needs.[4] I am convinced that future research will also demonstrate that people working under such conditions become more mature and creative individuals in their homes, in community life, and as citizens.

As a final example, let us examine some efforts to train people in workshops, institutes, and special training courses. Such efforts are common in various areas of social welfare, intergroup relations, political affairs, industry, and adult education. It is an unfortunate fact that objective evaluation of the effects of such training has only rarely been undertaken, but there is evidence that the change in participant behavior is most disappointing. A workshop not infrequently develops keen interest among the participants, high morale and enthusiasm, and a firm resolve on the part of many to apply all the wonderful insights back home. But what happens back home? The trainee discovers that his colleagues don't share his enthusiasm. He learns that the task of changing the expectations of others and their ways of doing things is discouragingly difficult. He senses, perhaps not very clearly, that it would make "all the difference in the world" if only there were a few other people sharing his insights, persons with whom he could plan activities, evaluate consequences of efforts, and from whom he could gain emotional and motivational support.

A few years ago the Research Center for Group Dynamics undertook to shed light on this problem by investigating the operation of a workshop for training leaders in intercultural

[4]L. Coch and J. R. P. French, Jr., "Overcoming Resistance to Change," *Human Relations*, 1 (1948), 512-532.

relations.[5] In a project, directed by Lippitt, we set out to compare systematically the different effects of the workshop upon trainees who came as *individuals* in contrast to those who came as *teams*. Since one of the problems in this field is that of getting people of good will to be more active in community efforts to improve intergroup relations, one goal of the workshop was to increase the activity of the trainees in local affairs. No difference could be found, prior to the workshop, in the community activities of persons who were to be trained as individuals and as teams. Six months after the workshop, however, those who had been trained as isolates were only slightly more active than before the workshop, whereas those who had been members of strong training teams were much more active. We do not have clear evidence on the point, but it appeared that the workshop was a "shot in the arm" for the isolates. For the team member, it produced more enduring changes because the team provided continuous support and reinforcement for its members.

THE GROUP AND SOCIAL CHANGE

What conclusions may we draw from these examples? What principles of achieving change in people appear to emerge? To begin with the most general proposition, we may state that the behavior, attitudes, beliefs, and values of an average person are firmly grounded in the groups to which he belongs. How aggressive or cooperative he is, how much self-respect and self-confidence he has, how energetic and productive his work, what he aspires to do, what he believes to be true and good, whom he loves or hates, the prejudices he holds—*all these characteristics are highly determined by the individual's group memberships.* In a real sense, they are properties of these groups, i.e., relationships among people. Whether

5Ronald Lippitt, *Training in Community Relations* (New York: Harper and Brothers, 1949).

persons change or resist change will, therefore, be greatly influenced by the nature of their groups. Attempts to change them must be concerned with the dynamics of groups.

In examining more specifically how groups enter into the process of change, it is useful to view groups in at least three ways. In the first view, the group is seen as a source of influence over its members. Efforts to change behavior can be supported or blocked by pressures on members stemming from the group. To make constructive use of these pressures the group must be used *as a medium of change.* In the second view, the group itself becomes the *target of change.* To change the behavior of individuals it may be necessary to change the standards of the group, its style of leadership, its emotional atmosphere, or its stratification into cliques and hierarchies. Even though the goal may be to change the behavior of individuals, the object of change becomes the group. In the third view, it is recognized that many changes of behavior can be brought about only by the organized efforts of groups *as agents of change.* A committee to combat intolerance, a labor union, an employers association, a citizens group to increase the pay of teachers—any action group will be more or less effective depending upon the way it is organized, the satisfactions it provides to its members, the degree to which its goals are clear, and a host of other properties of the group.

An adequate social technology of change, then, requires at the very least a scientific understanding of groups viewed in each of these ways. In the time remaining, I should like to propose some tentative principles concerning the effective utilization of the group, first, as *a medium of change.*

(1) If the group is to be used effectively as a medium of change, those people who are to be changed and those who are to exert influence for change must have a strong sense of belonging to the same group.

Kurt Lewin describes this principle well: "The normal gap between teacher and student, doctor and patient, social worker and public, can . . . be a real obstacle to acceptance of the advocated conduct. In other words, in spite of whatever status differences there might be between them, the teacher and the student have to feel as members of one group in matters involving their sense of values. The chances for re-education seem to be increased whenever a strong we-feeling is created."[6] Recent experiments by Preston and Heintz have demonstrated greater changes of opinions among members of discussion groups operating with participatory leadership than among those with supervisory leadership.[7] The implications of this principle for classroom teaching are far-reaching, the same may be said of supervision in, for example, a factory, the army, a hospital.

> (2) The more attractive the group is to its members the greater is the influence that the group can exert on its members.

This principle has been extensively documented by Festinger and his co-workers.[8] They have been able to show in a variety of settings that in more cohesive groups there is a greater readiness of members to attempt to influence others, a greater readiness to be influenced by others, and stronger pressures toward conformity when conformity is a relevant matter for the group. Important for the practitioner is, of course, the question of how to increase the attractiveness of

[6]Kurt Lewin, *Resolving Social Conflicts* (New York: Harper and Brothers, 1948), p. 67.

[7]M. G. Preston and R. K. Heintz, "Effects of Participatory vs. Supervisory Leadership on Group Judgment," *The Journal of Abnormal and Social Psychology*, 44 (1949), 345-355.

[8]Leon Festinger *et al.*, *Theory and Experiment in Social Communication: Collected Papers* (Ann Arbor: Institute for Social Research, 1950).

groups. Suffice it to say that, obviously, a group is more attractive the more it satisfies the needs of its members. We have been able to demonstrate experimentally an increase in group cohesiveness by increasing the liking of members for each other, by increasing the perceived importance of the group goal, and by increasing the prestige of the group among other groups. Experienced group workers can add many other procedures.

> (3) In attempts to change attitudes, values, or behavior, the more relevant these are to the basis of attraction to the group, the greater will be the influence that the group can exert upon them.

I believe this principle gives a clue to some otherwise puzzling phenomena. How does it happen that a group, for instance, a labor union, seems to be able to exert such strong discipline over its members in some matters, (let us say in dealings with management) while it seems unable to exert anything like the same influence in other matters, say in political action? If one examines why it is that members are attracted to the group, he will find that particular reasons for belonging are more related to some of the group's activities than to others. If a man joins a union mainly to keep his job and to improve his working conditions, he may be largely uninfluenced by the union's attempt to modify his attitudes toward national and international affairs. Groups differ tremendously in the range of matters that are relevant to their members and, hence, over which they have influence. Adult education could be improved by paying attention to this principle.

> (4) The greater the prestige of a group member in the eyes of the other members, the greater the influence he can exert.

Lippitt, Polansky, and Redl[9] have demonstrated this prin-

[9] N. Polansky, R. Lippitt, and F. Redl, "An Investigation of Behavioral Contagion in Groups," *Human Relations,* 3 (1950), 319-348.

ciple with great care and methodological ingenuity in a series of studies in children's summer camps. From a practical point of view it must be emphasized that the things giving prestige to a member may not be those characteristics most prized by the official management of the group. The most prestigeful member of a Sunday School class may not possess the characteristics most similar to the minister of the church. The teacher's pet may be a poor source of influence within a class. This principle is the basis for the common observation that the official leader and the actual leader of a group are often not the same individual.

(5) Efforts to change individuals or subparts of a group which, if successful, would have the result of making them deviate from the norms of the group will encounter strong resistance.

During the past few years a great deal of evidence has been accumulated showing the tremendous pressure which groups can exert upon members to conform to the group's norms. The price of deviation in most groups is rejection or even expulsion. If the member really wants to belong and be accepted, he can scarcely withstand this type of influence. It is for this reason that efforts to change people by taking them from the group and giving them special training so often have disappointing results. This principle also accounts for the finding that people thus trained sometimes display increased tension, aggressiveness toward the group, or a tendency to form cults or cliques with others who have shared their training.

These five principles concerning the group as a medium of change would appear to have readiest application to groups created for the purpose of producing changes in people. They provide certain specifications for building effective training or therapy groups. They also point, however, to a difficulty in producing change in people in that they show how resistant an individual is to changing in any way contrary to group pressures and expectations. In order to achieve many kinds of changes in people, therefore, it is necessary to deal with the groups as *a target of change.*

(6) Strong pressure for changes in the group can be established by creating a shared perception by members of the need for change, thus making the source of pressure for change lie within the group.

Marrow and French[10] report a dramatic case-study which illustrates this principle quite well. A manufacturing company had a policy against hiring women over thirty because it was believed that they were slower, more difficult to train, and more likely to be absent. The staff psychologist was able to present to management evidence that this belief was clearly unwarranted at least within that company. The psychologist's facts, however, were rejected as a basis for action. It was claimed the findings went against the direct experience of the foremen. Then the psychologist hit upon a plan for achieving change; namely, he proposed that management conduct its own analysis of the situation. With his help management collected all the facts which they believed relevant, making them their facts rather than those of an outside expert, and policy was altered without undue resistance. The important point is that "facts" are not enough. They must be the accepted property of the group if they are to become an effective basis for change.

(7) Information relating to the need for change, plans for change, and consequences of change must be shared by all relevant people in the group.

Another way of stating this principle is to say that change in a group ordinarily requires the opening up of communication

[10]A. J. Marrow and J. R. P. French, Jr., "Changing a Stereotype in Industry," *Journal of Social Issues,* 1, No. 3 (1945), 33-37.

channels. Newcomb[11] has shown how one of the first consequences of mistrust and hostility is the avoidance of communicating openly and freely about the things producing the tension. If you will show me a pathological group, one that has trouble making decisions or coordinating member efforts, it is fairly certain that I can show you strong restraints in that group against communicating vital information. Until these restraints are removed there can be little hope for any real and lasting changes in the group's functioning. In passing, it should be pointed out that the removal of barriers to communication will ordinarily be accompanied by a sudden increase in the communication of hostility. The group may appear to be falling apart, and it will certainly be a painful experience to many of the members. This pain, and the fear that things are getting out of hand, may stop the process of change.

(8) Changes in one part of a group produce strain in other related parts which can be reduced only by eliminating the change or by bringing about readjustments in the related parts.

It is a common practice to undertake improvements in group functioning by providing training programs for certain classes of people in the organization. For example, a training program for nurses is established. If the content of training is relevant for organizational change, it must of necessity deal with the relationships that nurses have with other subgroups, such as doctors and patients. It is unrealistic to assume that these latter groups will remain indifferent to changes in the nurses. On the contrary, their tendency will be to re-establish the old equilibrium, to negate the changes.

These eight principles represent a few of the basic propositions emerging from research in group dynamics. Since re-

[11]T. M. Newcomb, "Autistic Hostility and Social Reality," *Human Relations,* 1 (1947), 69-86.

search is constantly going on and since its very nature is to revise its conceptions, we may be sure that these principles will have to be modified and improved as time passes. In the meantime they may serve as guides in our endeavors to develop a scientifically based technology of social management.

In social technology, just as in physical technology, *invention* plays a crucial role. In both fields progress consists of the creation of new mechanisms for the accomplishment of certain goals. Inventions arise in response to practical needs and are to be evaluated by how effectively they satisfy these needs. While inventions will be more effective the more they make use of known principles of science, they are in no sense logical derivations from scientific principles. They cannot proceed too far ahead of basic scientific development, nor should they be allowed to fall too far behind.

I have taken this brief excursion into the theory of invention in order to make a final point. To many people "group dynamics" is known only for the social inventions which have developed in recent years in work with groups. Role-playing, buzz groups, process observers, post-meeting reaction sheets, and feedback of group observations are devices popularly associated with the phrase "group dynamics." I trust that I have been able to show that group dynamics is more than a collection of gadgets. It certainly aspires to be a science as well as a technology.

This is not to underplay the importance of these inventions nor of the function of inventing. As inventions they are all mechanisms designed to help accomplish important goals. How effective they are will depend upon how skillfully they are used and how appropriate they are to the purposes to which they are put. Careful evaluative research must be the ultimate judge of their usefulness in comparison to alternative inventions. I believe the principles enumerated here indicate some specifications that social inventions in this field must meet.

CHAPTER 5

Intergroup Relations— The Educator's Role

LLOYD ALLEN COOK

Professor of Education, Wayne University; formerly Director of the National College Study in Intergroup Relations.

LLOYD ALLEN COOK

Intergroup Relations—
The Educator's Role

WITH THIS LECTURE, we conclude the first annual
Leo M. Franklin Lectures in Human Relations, public discussions in honor of a great teacher. It was intended that the series
would have some unity, that it would deal with some problems
of these times. The first lecture was foundational, treating freedom, power and value conflicts. The second developed a
dynamic idea of democracy, urging its empirical test. The next
two discussed phases of purposive change making, the assumption being that this was the heart of the human relations issue.
I propose to continue this latter theme, to draw some materials
from College Study experience and to interpret them.

The College Study in Intergroup Relations was a cooperative effort to improve teacher education, national in scope and
of four years duration.[1] It was under the auspices of the American Council on Education and was financed by a grant from the
National Conference of Christians and Jews. It involved a
number of colleges and universities, along with their related

[1]See Lloyd Allen Cook, ed., *College Programs in Intergroup Relations* and, as author, *Intergroup Relations in Teacher Education*
(Washington: American Council on Education, 1950, 1951).

schools, goodwill agencies, and civic groups. Project aims, as they evolved, came to include six major goals.

1. To make factual studies of inter- and intra-group relations in the areas of race, creed, national cultures, and social class, using the techniques of modern psycho-social inquiry.

2. To assess study findings in light of personality needs and equal-rights values, with particular concern for equality of opportunity in child, youth and adult life.

3. Where undesirable and unhealthful conditions are found, to initiate ameliorative change action, focusing especially on prejudice and discrimination.

4. To develop programs in preservice teacher education which will prepare prospective teachers for effective work in the field of intergroup relations.

5. To cooperate with local, state and national inter-group agencies, mayor's committees, etc., offering them technical help on educational problems, as well as citizen support.

6. To interpret group-relations work to educators, to community leaders and the public, advancing it as a respected area in the training of lay and professional persons.

COLLEGE STUDY CHANGE PROJECTS

College Study files contain data on 379 concrete efforts to realize the above goals, to teach better human relations within some specific context. These are only the cases that are clear enough in design, and complete enough in findings, to permit evaluation. In 26 of these, experimenters had pre- and end-test data on attitudinal and other changes. In 92 cases, assessment was made from cumulative file material, chiefly reports of project directors, our own regular field visits, participant ratings and self reports. In the remainder of the 379 cases, data are much as just described except that they are less complete. Table 1 is an overall estimate of this work.

TABLE 1
Impressions of Success or Failure in Change Projects*

	All Projects	No Change Evident	Some Change	Basic Change
1. In course content, purposes	83	22	37	24
2. In teaching methods.....	68	9	43	16
3. In extracurricular activities	64	5	23	36
4. In guidance and personnel work	20	2	6	12
5. In practice teaching, student experience	34	6	10	18
6. In school-community relations, area changes.......	37	16	12	9
7. In workshops for teachers and others	44	30	..	14
8. In college and school policy, records	12	..	4	8
9. In miscellaneous areas....	17	4	7	6
Total..........	379	94	142	143

*From *Intergroup Relations in Teacher Education,* p. 84.

What Table 1 suggests is that about two-thirds of the projects studied did pay off. While these activities differ in ways that no brief comment can make clear, the main work unit was the small study-action group. In the four-year period, 226 of these "teams" were listed in college reports. These groups ranged from two to forty members, averaging about six, and they met in all over 2,000 times. They consisted mostly of students and faculty at college and public school levels, plus in half the cases community representatives. Some groups had a life span of a semester or less, whereas others—over a fourth —were at work from two years to four. In addition to these routine, undramatic work efforts, every college in the program put on special events. At times these events were as large as the New York State Student Conference on Intergroup Relations, at the state teachers college, Albany, with an average daily attendance of 1,000 students, college and school faculty, townspeople, and others.

Of course, no field project can have the exactness demanded by rigorous experimentalists, yet it is interesting to compare the table just cited with the most precise work on record. After a thorough search of the literature, Rose found 66 college and school studies in prejudice reduction. His appraisal of success or failure is as follows:

TABLE 2
Experimental Efforts to Reduce Prejudice*

Influence Studied	Total	Change	No Change	Indefinite
1. School or college course...	13	8	4	1
2. Mass media such as films, radio	14	9	4	1
3. Correlation studies, knowledge (or acquaintance) with attitudes	12	9	2	1
4. Years spent at school or college	18	8	6	4
5. Personalized contacts, trips, visits	9	3	3	3
Total	66	37	19	10

Well over half the studies appraised in Table 2 showed reductions in prejudices or, better said, a growth in friendly, liberal attitudes and understanding. *Education can change people, a conclusion on which no educator in school or college, or outside, need ever be in serious doubt.*

What kinds of teaching methods are most effective? Frankly, we do not believe that anyone has as yet any conclusive

*Adapted from Arnold Rose, *Studies in the Reduction of Prejudice* (Chicago: American Council on Race Relations, 1948), p. 18.

answer. The main reasons for this uncertainty are (1) the near impossibility of singling out one factor, teaching, in a multi-factor complex, and (2) the difficulty of establishing exact situational controls. To be certain, there has been—and increasingly is—excellent work in this field, some fully approximating Allport's ideal design. But we have seen too much teaching to count this issue closed. Good teachers tend to get good results with "poor" methods, and bad teachers fail with the best methods we know. Teacher personality is a basic variable, one hard to control in an experimental plan.

While, to us, the above case is still open, the weight of evidence is beginning to point in certain ways. The strength of academic teaching, our most dominant and traditional method, lies in the learning of factual content, such as concepts and principles. For changing perceptions and attitudes, we favor the cooperative "group process" approach where participants function as a study-action team, making area trips and using audiovisual materials as the need arises. This same method is effective in teaching human relations skills. In respect to direct vs. indirect ways of classroom teaching, the evidence is still conflicting, as it is also in mass media (propaganda) research.

A LITTLE MORE, A LITTLE BETTER, PLANNING

How is one to communicate to teachers, church and agency workers, civic leaders and lay persons, what really went on in College Study work? While we do not know the answer and, too, tastes will differ, some actual look-see examples might be of use. The incidents I shall select from our file of some 5,000 cases are purely random, having no purpose except to show the effort made to solve some particular problem involving race, creed, or the like.

In general, school teachers have had no college course in intergroup relations, no special training for this work. Their problems may come as a complete surprise, descending upon them on the job. Often a little more thought, a little more planning, might have brought better results.

The first case is that of a white teacher in an ungraded school for Negro boys. I present it in his words.

WHY I WANT A TRANSFER

Last spring, our school gave a musical show. A visiting principal from a nearby school invited us to repeat the show at his school. Since his community is white, we felt that we could strike a lick for better race relations as well as help this school get money for a band and glee club. Our faculty accepted the invitation when the suburban principal offered to provide our boys with bus transportation.

My principal asked me to take charge, and I explained the project to the boys. I told them we were to repeat the show, no changes, just what we had done. I said we should behave like gentlemen on this visit for we would be judged by our conduct as well as by our music. I asked them to meet for the trip at 5:30 p.m. on the scheduled date, when the busses would come for us. They were to tell their parents that these busses would return us about ten o'clock that evening, all of which seemed to be o.k. with the boys.

Every boy showed up and we got away on time. We had been told to go to the school gym, where we found that pupils and parents were eating a school supper. While they had not counted on us, we were given tables and fed. Our show went off fine, in fact was a big success. . . . The show, we saw, was to be followed by a dance, and an orchestra tuned up. Since we had about a half hour to kill, I told the boys that we would watch the dance but not, ourselves, participate unless we were invited.

Everything was smooth until ten o'clock, when the

busses came. Two of the boys did not want to go home, offering to hitchhike their way. At first I talked with them, and then I made them board a bus. I noticed that a number of them were rather sullen on the way home.

Next morning at class, I had rebellion. One pupil asked me why I had made the boys leave the dance, and I said that the busses were scheduled to meet us at ten o'clock. He said that I was "prejudiced," that I was against the boys having any fun, all of which I denied. He said that his mother was coming to talk with the principal, which she did that afternoon. When I explained again about the bus, she said that this was no excuse for my action, that the boys could have gotten home. She charged also that I was prejudiced, telling the principal in my presence that I should be fired.

In class next day, I told the boys about this conference. They said again that I did not like colored pupils, that I did not think they were as good as whites. I did not get mad until they asked me about my daughter. They asked if, when she grew up, would she be allowed to date a Negro boy. I replied, "No, of course not," explaining that mixed dating was no good for either race. They said now that I had convicted myself of prejudice, that they were going to run me out of school.

More parents came in and complained about me. I think also a man from the NAACP called on the principal. Pupils were openly disrespectful, slacking off in their work, causing trouble in little ways. Nothing like this had existed before the bus trip. . . . The Negro counselor and several teachers of both races tried to stop this, for they knew that I was not prejudiced. I had come to this school at my own request. Now, I have been forced to change my mind. While I am asking for help on this problem, I have also applied for a school transfer. I cannot do good work in the present situation and I do not know how to change it.

About half our cases are of this sort—trouble cases where conflict is in process. In the case at issue, the point is not whether the teacher is prejudiced, for the evidence is incomplete. What is clear is that this teacher ignored the risks inherent in the bus-trip, the kinds of foreseeable outcomes which should have been guarded against. He did no real planning with the boys, merely transmitting the principal's orders. He had, therefore, only the weight of his office in enforcing the going-home rule. More hazardous still were the interracial eating and dancing situations, prime danger spots in a good many places. The teacher had not been briefed on these, nor did he make any effort to secure data on which group planning could have been done. His handling of the charge of "prejudice" was naive, assuming he wanted to clear himself.

THE NEED FOR EVIDENCE

There is nothing mystical about group process teaching, nothing to justify the near awe and reverence with which at times it is discussed. Its essence is to estimate a situation, to think through alternative courses of action, to sound out a group as to its preferences and start to work. One needs evidence on which to act, and a crucial problem is what kinds of data to collect. While systematic study is to be recommended, the value of pick-up data should not be ignored. For example, I can recall a lot of fancy figures on a current school-community case, statistics anyone might admire. But when the group cam to make an action plan, planners were far more impressed witl. pupil stories about area life. The sample given is a paper written as an in-class assignment by a 4B girl. Spelling is somewhat original, yet meanings are never in doubt.

WHAT MY NEIGHBOR IS LIKE

I sure think in this neighbor that the mens chase girls to much because you can't go into streets at night if'n you got no pertection. Because, like I said, some dirty ol' rat will grab you and feel you, and everyplace all over. And you can't go to resterant where whites will say, no, not allow you coloreds. And you can't find a decent job, you know for pay work. Prices here are terrible. . . .

I think this that we people should complain about. These here houses are dirty broken down. And they is full of bugs, and all kind of things not fit for children to live in. All kinds of things and rats around. And the streets is bars and stuff, drunks and fightings going on. Mens are drunk or not and see them usin' trees just like dog messes. . . . Whites is worse I think but I don't know if they worse than coloreds. They is unfit to live in the United States of America but fit to live in Russia. . . .

I don't think there is any wrong with the school. Some teachers we got horde supplies we got to work with. . . . Excep' for boys. They treat you jest like they owne you. They grabs you jest like the mens, and they should be dead also.

In these scrawly writings of alley-wise kids, one gets a feel for slum-area life, the forces shaping child personality. Here is sex in its vicious forms; dirt, hunger, bad housing, crime. One finds, in fact, many kinds of data, for children stray from this to that—a communal cat, some sparkling bit of jewelry, a "bustes-fit" sweater. Whites figure in these stories by Negro children, at times in brutal ways but mostly as just "mean." Often, boys rate white teachers as "real swell," and girls express the wish to touch their clothes or hold their hands.

Other kinds of quick-take data come to mind, each a way of sizing up a situation. Our point is not to argue against formal study, for every science-minded person is dependent on it. It is rather to urge that we get some data on which to work, the best data we can. No individual, and no group, should be stampeded into a "do something" program until it is decided what to do. Usually, a guess must be made, an hypothesis advanced, as to what action to take, what will likely happen in case of this or that. There is no certainty, only *probability*, as in all science, all art and practice.

WORKING WITH A SCHOOL STAFF

Often, in conflict resolution, one ponders where to take hold, to try to re-establish communication in a house divided against itself. The problem with which the next case deals is that of a mixed Negro-white school staff. I had been asked to address the faculty on extracurricular activities, to speak particularly on why, in other places, students and faculty had lost interest in these activities.

A SCHOOL CONFLICT CASE

Arriving at the school an hour or so ahead of meeting time, I heard noises in the gym. A look inside showed a basketball game. Three white boys were teamed against two Negro boys, with no one else in sight. Presently, a Negro student came in and joined the Negro players, evening the count. Two white boys came along, making a five-man white team against the three colored players. Another white came in and was held in reserve. With such odds against them, the Negro boys could not do much. About this time, a commotion broke out outside the gym, and we all rushed to the ground-level window to see what was going on. A fight was on, but, before we could get through the window, a Negro janitor had pulled the battlers apart and scattered the crowd of boys and girls who had gathered.

What had happened could be pretty well pieced out. A white teacher had come walking down the narrow cement walk from the main building to the gym. She was met head on by a rather large Negro girl. "I ain't gonna let you by," the girl had said. "Now, Bessie," the teacher had replied, "I'm in a hurry and I want to pass." The girl repeated her statement, not budging from the center of the walk. When the teacher tried to push past, she was shoved off the cement. Stepping back, she either pushed or slapped Bessie, who hit back, causing the teacher to fall to the ground. At this point, the janitor ran out and stopped the fight.

After things had settled down, I went on in to see the principal. Still seeking evidence on the nature of human nature in this school, I offered to finish a period for an art teacher who had suddenly taken ill. As I entered this classroom, a whisper of "sub, sub" went over the group, a comment that any substitute teacher can fully understand. After facing the class a minute or two, with no indication that students were going to quiet down, I turned away from the group and walked to the blackboard. Anything could have happened—crayons or ink might have come sailing up, a risk it seemed necessary to run.

Taken unawares, the group did focus on the sketch that I was drawing, a crude picture of a comic-strip character. Asked to identify this fellow, several students shouted a reply. Asked if anyone could take the chalk and give the guy the arm muscles which are his trademark, a student volunteered. After this was over, I began another sketch. The group was attentive until, in the silence, there came a strong, coarse voice. "You funny, funny man. If you think we-all are gonna laugh at them funny, funny pitures, you can kiss our ——." Everybody laughed, including the teacher, as he turned to face the class. The girl who had spoken made no effort to conceal her identity, so that a question was directed to her. Would she come up and complete the sketch? Her reply was that "she didn't do nothin' for no white man!"

At the faculty meeting shortly, I was introduced to speak on extracurricular activities, a topic quickly broadened to include the human relations of the school. After a few minutes, we came to the point. What was the school's No. 1 problem in human relations, the problem on which it most needed help? No one spoke, and the query was repeated. Again silence. On a third trial, I stepped directly in front of the principal and spoke to him, counting on him to assume his usual rôle as faculty spokesman. He did not want any teacher, he said, to name a problem for "the problem should be group determined." He went on to say that a committee should be appointed, which he did, and the meeting was adjourned.

Two weeks later, we met again. Had the committee done its work? Its chairman's reply was strongly positive. Had all the faculty members been canvassed? Had responses been counted and put in order? Yes, to both questions. What, then, was the No. 1 human relations problem of the school? It was, in a word, "the chewing of chewing gum!" Bubble gum, the chairman added, was the worst, a sticky business at best.

What now, is an adult to do with adults at such moments? Is he to bawl them out, treat them like irresponsible children? Is he to ask them, kindly but firmly, to face reality, knowing that they cannot? No one had laughed when the committee report was made, in fact the atmosphere was tense. Everyone knew what the real problem was, knew that education could not get on because it could not get over the fact of race. And yet here we were, able persons in our several ways, stuck on a wad of chewing gum!

Trying to get my wits together, I remarked that this was the first time I had ever had a problem like this . . . and so forth. What, now, were we to do? How could gum chewing be stopped? Little by little, fearful and hesitant, teachers began to talk. The upshot was a conventional school campaign—assembly announcements, homeroom talks, hall posters, notes to parents, and the like.

About a month later, I was again invited to the school, this time to hear a progress report. The news was definitely bad. Apparently, little progress had been made and, in some ways, the situation worsened. Students were chewing gum who had never chewed before. Moreover, the faculty felt no sense of failure, for no one had much believed that anything could be done. The battle had not been lost; it simply had not been fought.

The time had come, I thought, to arouse these teachers, stir them up, get them into action. . . . Maybe the kids were smarter than we had thought. Maybe they ran the school, told the staff what to do. Maybe teachers only worked here, punching the time clock, maybe . . . maybe . . . with insinuation piled on insinuation. No person who is a person can stand this very long, this cumulative ego insult. Sooner or later, he will come alive, rise up and take command. This is exactly what began to happen to this school staff. Who did the professor think he was? By what right did he go around insulting people? Had he ever been outside of academic halls, taught in a race-ridden school?

To all of this, I offered no counter argument, no opposition. Presently, we all began to cool down, a little ashamed of our respective roles. Faced now with a deepening sense of failure, we agreed that the chewing-gum problem was a tough one, that we would have to get together to get it solved. Why were students so resistant, so adamant about the matter? Was gum-chewing significant in itself or merely symbolical? Did it really show an anti-faculty point of view? How did kids get status in the school? What kind of group codes were we up against? Who were the popular students, the ones others patterned on? Could we find them through sociometric study. Could we come, in time, to lead through the natural leaders of the school?

We shall leave the case at this point, though there is much more to it. Once the great to-do about gum-chewing subsided, students lost interest in the art. Of course, they broke out in other ways, but by now the faculty had begun to wise up. For the first time, I would guess, staff members had become concerned about the total school, its shortcomings and potentialities. Moreover, one could sense a growing firmness of viewpoint, the beginning unity of a common cause. This work is still in process, and race is not quite the bugaboo that it was.

If this case supports any moral, it is the simple thought that the *function of leadership is to lead.* It is not to hold hands, a current theory of group work, or to wave flags, or make speeches. It is not to do nothing, or to find good reasons why nothing can be done. It is not to wait for time to solve problems, or to engage in juvenile inanities, or to spread screens for covert actions. It is to help people help themselves out of jams, to point them toward whatever sensible goals they may judge possible, knowing that as a group acts under guidance it will grow stronger in its potentials for further action. There is, in all democratic education, a considerable faith in process, the kind of process to which Cartwright's principles apply.

Before leaving school cases, it is well to post a caution. A reader may say: "But I don't understand. Why are you so critical of our schools? Aren't they any good?" Yes, they are good, maybe the best the nation has ever had. They are, for certain, about as good as they can be, considering the work they have to do and the support they get. But schools are not perfect, and no one who knows them would claim so. In human relations, we all have a lot to learn and we ought to learn it as fast as possible. Thus, in any case-oriented paper, the focus is bound to be on atypical situations where good teaching is absent, where unclarity and/or inaction rule. It would take a thoughtless critic to draw inferences from such "trouble spots" about public education as a whole.

SOME COMMUNITY CASES

Group process education goes on in the community as well as in the school. At times the problem is a food-clothing-shelter issue; at times less tangible rights, needs, or interests. Here is a small public meeting in an average smalltown:

TAKING A LOOK AT OUR TOWN

At this community meeting, the people had been divided by age levels. Young children sat in one section of the school auditorium, adolescents in another, young adults in a third, elders in a fourth. After introductions, it was explained that few communities are perfect, that most places want to improve themselves, that a public audit was one way of assessing strengths and weaknesses. With this, I wrote on a big blackboard these questions:

Our Town

1. What is good about it?
2. What needs to be done?
3. Who can undertake this?
4. What will it cost?
5. When can it be begun?
6. How can I help out?

The idea was to move back and forth across the hall, taking statements from each section. Of all the age levels, the little children provided the most excitement. They passed their first turn, unable to state a problem, but on the second round a little girl threw the audience into an uproar.

This girl, a precocious fifth grader, stood up and said she had a problem. Asked to state it, she said the town was "corrupt." Not sure that I had understood, I asked the child to repeat. Once again the youngster said the town was "corrupt," and once again the audience howled. On a split second decision, it seemed best not to go into this issue, a bad mistake on my part, and so we asked for the next problem. . . .

As the meeting broke up, down the aisle came a distraught mother, her little daughter very much in hand. "Stop the people, Professor." . . . "Tell him, Ellen." . . . "Stop the people." . . . A big mistake had been made, and it had to be corrected. In reading the local paper that evening, Ellen had met a word she did not understand; and papa, busy with his own reading, did not really hear her question. The town was not "corrupt" but "bankrupt," or so its trustees said. Once this was cleared up with the departing audience, the only casualty was the little girl, crying softly to herself.

Several good things came out at that meeting. For example, a high school boy said that he lived about eight miles out in the country, that his parents wanted to attend the meeting but that the roads were too bad. A county official spoke on this subject, answering the questions raised. By arrangement, the newspaper editor was present and his paper ran a full account of the main discussions.

In general, people like this type of meeting. It should be focused on material lacks and wants rather than on complex human problems. While it is no better than its management, it can function to get thought started, to channel ideas toward persons in position to act, and to keep the public informed. As an educative experience for young people, what the town is like, how its big and little wheels go 'round, there is much to recommend the community audit. One can at times cut deeply into the civic ignorance of youth, their feelings of shut-outness and unconcern, their inability to get into any civic project that seems to matter.

In view of the great popularity of role playing, I should perhaps cite a case of this kind. Role taking (sociodrama) can be a faddish bit of nonsense, or it can become an effective educational technique. We have used it mostly in skill training, for instance, in the conduct of public meetings, in doorbell pushing campaigns, in the management of classrooms.

The case below grows out of a concern of long standing. Over the nation, there are thousands of public-minded citizens who do yeoman service as board members of voluntary socio-civic organizations. I mean service clubs, lodges, churches, school boards, P.T.A.'s, women's clubs, and the like. Few of these persons have had any particular training for the work they do, and if any help is possible, they are entitled to it.

A BOARD-MEMBER CLINIC, ROLE TAKING

In a middle-states city, a two-day "problem-clinic" was called for directors of local sociocivic, religious and educational organizations. It was held under joint college and community auspices, and attendance increased from about 400 at the first session to over 600 at the last session.

In brief opening remarks, it was explained how every community depends on its many civic bodies, that democracy functions through them even as it does through governmental offices, that few board members have had any special training for their various functions. The purpose of the conference was to look into the training problem, to provide board members help if that was possible.

How do board members get their jobs? When someone started to answer, he was invited to come to a small, central platform, to take a seat at the table and discuss the matter with us. Three college students, each coached in a part, sat at the table. The real board-member's job was "to show us, not tell us" how the selection process actually takes place.

This session brought, of course, a good many laughs, for the college students invented all sorts of kibitzing tactics. As the simulated board meeting went on, other board members were drawn into it. Presently a woman spoke from the audience to say that her church board did not behave that way, that the selection of new board members was made outside of meeting and simply announced there. This led to several efforts to show what these common practices were, though this was skating on pretty thin ice. After several improvisations, the audience was asked to react to what had been done. Were we realistic? Could present practices be improved? What kind of person makes a good board member?

Other sessions during the two days dealt with other phases of board member behavior, for instance, the process of decision making. The last session in particular was notable. It was on the rewards and costs to individuals of unpaid board membership. We were lucky in having present an elderly businessman, a respected patriarch, who took to heart the task of summing up a lifetime of civic goodwill work, the satisfactions he had found in services to state, county and town.

At no time in such meetings are people pressed beyond the reality level at which they feel comfortable, and fun is mixed with business in a way that can pack an auditorium. Where several sessions are held, one may be besieged with bids to private talks, with phone calls and letters, letting him in on the scandals of the town. This is a fairly good sign that a program is taking hold, that it is moving toward pay dirt. Needless to say, such material must be held in confidence and used, if at all, only as a general guide to professional work.

SUCCESS OR FAILURE, TEST CASE

Among college cases, perhaps a third deal with what I shall presently call human rights education. I shall pass these cases in favor of two less routine examples. The first presents the problem of what group process education is, how to get it started. The scene is a Southern university where we had been asked to demonstrate sociodrama to a graduate class.

THE PROBLEM OF EDUCATIVE ACTION

After a very brief statement had been made, a panel of students was assembled, each student being a teacher or a principal in the area. Again, to save time, I spoke about the then current and much debated report of the President's Committee entitled *To Secure These Rights*. I asked if some panel member could see an interracial issue in this report.

When no one spoke, we went at the report again. Again there was silence. Allowing time, I repeated the request but still no student could think of any racial issue. The group favored segregated education. It felt that federal school-aid funds should not be equalized and that, all things considered, Negro education was in good shape. With time going, we felt compelled to leave race. We quickly picked up a genuine difference of opinion within the panel and went on to demonstrate sociodrama.

On the way out that evening, the professor in charge of the class chided us on our failure to get an interracial issue stated, implying that his own experience at the college had been much the same. I admitted that our performance did indeed look like failure but that we might wait and see if anything further happened.

Next morning, two panel members phoned for an appointment to "talk over some problems." At noon that day in the college dining hall, another participant in the evening program sat down at our table. His first remark was that "the meeting had been good, very good." Asked what was good about it, he was noncommittal. Pressed on this, he replied in all seriousness: "Well, you know how it is. We don't think too much of damn-Yanks down here. . . . You are the first one we can remember who has not come to reform us, to tell us how to solve the race problem."

At a group meeting that afternoon, this same student introduced, at his own volition, a genuine interracial problem. It involved a service study of some Negro school children, hence was well within the mores of the white South. To study Negroes, or to help them, does not violate the caste line as would, for example, working and planning with Negroes to solve some common problem.

Was this first evening at the college a failure? If its chief aim was to get thought started on race relations, it failed to do this. Must one win the right to work with people, to invade their areas or privacy? If the change desired is in conduct, *must education in human relations be a self-willed act?* If so, how does one induce this voluntary participation? By a war of mind on mind, a piling up of fact and logic? By appeal, by pressure, by warm personal relations? By providing experience in real-life action processes? Race-oriented talk did grow up at this Southern college over a year's time, a great deal of it. But it has not yet reached the level where some university students would begin their thought.

SHOCK TACTICS, A LAST RESORT

The case I wish to use now may seem strange in light of what has been said. The setting is again the South, a small college for Negroes with a mixed Negro and white staff. The faculty takes pride in its radicalism, its all-out war on the caste system, its no-compromise stand. Let me take some incidents from another man's story, look at happenings through his eyes.

My reference is to an unusual College Study document, a year-long private diary, written for his own reasons by a participant in the local program. Except for deletions, diary quotes are exact. The present writer is the "Dr. C" in the case, also the "CS director."

COMMUNICATION—BREAKDOWN AND REPAIR

Oct. 6. All hands present to hear Dr. C on the College Study. Said much the same as we have read in his canned stuff. Interested in "democratic human relations," etc. Spoke too long and said too little for we know better than he ever will what the South is like. . . . But what the heck, we had voted to go into this project. . . . Another Boy Scout goodwill tour. . . .

Oct. 7. Small group meetings scheduled with the CS director. Much talk about what our college should try to do, the year's program. Three faculty members and two students at a meeting in my office. One prof quite impossible for anybody to work with. C listened to ideas, contributing very few of his own. Seemed reluctant to evaluate ours. Says he needs to catch the feel of the campus, our general mode of thought. . . .

Faculty met that evening at the J-home [president's home], and I am sure this meeting had been rigged. Not sure the CS guy had a hand in it, though he had eaten supper with the J-family. The president led off with his usual stale joke, followed by his usual pep talk. After this, our general chairman announced seven projects, asking each of us to take part in some one. He asked also that each group meet during the coming week, make a work plan and submit a budget of expenses.

I must say that C did not seem overly pleased at all this easy sailing, in fact seemed suspicious of it. He asked several times if enough thought had been given to the year's work, if the faculty felt certain of its general goals.

He cited other colleges in the Study where a quick survey of problems or needs had been made, followed by a discussion of priority demands. . . . But none of us wanted to open up, to tilt against the power alignments in this college. So the meeting closed.

Our perception of events during these first two days agrees very well with the views of the diary writer. We knew that staff members like him were seasoned veterans in race affairs, suspicious of a white outsider. We knew that factions existed on the campus, that a power group was backing the president's desire for participation in the College Study. Aside from suggesting a self survey for planning uses, we knew of nothing much to do. Our guess was that the college had a real action potential, that things might have to get worse before they could get any better, an estimate that proved fairly sound.

Oct. 16. Well, the fat is in the fire. I have, personally, organized opposition to the research projects foisted upon us. These projects are not in line with our needs and they call for time and skills that we do not have. We upset the applecart at a general committee meeting this evening. Voted the projects down, whereupon the president asked our side to prepare a new list of activities on which to work. . . .

These developments were communicated to us via letter from the deposed general chairman, a man whose place had been taken by the diary writer. On our next visit to the campus, we found five study-action groups at work. All but one of the old projects had been discarded and new ones devised, a change for the better in our judgment. Here we shall skip several pages in the diary in order to get at the crisis which was pending.

Nov. 4. C came in this morning and will meet for two days with our five groups. Said some things in chapel we do not like. Met with some students to show off "role playing," the big idea being to keep communication going across racial lines (baloney!). Met this afternoon with three groups, advising them on their plans. The guy is not much help to us for he takes a compromise stand. "Get what you can," he says, "then try to get more," and we do not go for that. We do not fight race battles that way. It is equal rights or none for us, a lesson we shall have to teach our visitor in the hard way.

Took a walk with C after the last meeting. He asked how the day's work had gone. "Not good," I said. He said he knew he had not been doing well and wondered why. I let him have it but good. . . . He replied with equal frankness . . . saying that his views seemed to clash with our student-faculty thought. I told him about our anti-caste stand, anti-compromise, anti-everything else. . . . We kicked this around a bit, back and forth. C asked then if I knew a good consultant the college would like to have, saying he would provide the cash. Now, what can you do with a guy like that! I told him "No, we had not given him up," that we would "save him yet." We both laughed at this and let the matter drop.

I felt at this point that the job was too much for me, that the need was for a competent man, thus the offer to seek the services of any consultant the college might want. When the general committee chairman, the diary writer, turned down this proposal, it seemed time to rethink the situation. My decision was to stick it out, to make one final try. After discarding several ideas, a vague sort of plan was shaped up.

Nov. 4. [Cont'd.] Supper that evening at my home and the usual bull session. Eight faculty members present, two white. Things dull, nothing to talk about. C started telling experiences in another Negro college. Nobody much interested. C told of an argument in a bull session. Said some prof had said that no white person could tell a Negro Joke to a Negro audience and not give offense. Prof L said "very interesting, *very* interesting," sarcastic as the devil, and C got the point. . . .

C then really spilled the beans. Told a joke he thought was funny but would give no offense. Said he got on a bus in Detroit, took a seat behind two small Negro boys. Listening to their gab, he heard the bigger one say: "How ol' is you?" "Dunno," the other boy said. "Dunno how ol' yo' is," the first boy repeated. "Naw," from his pal. "Well, den, is yo' fouh or is yo' five?" "Is ah fouh or is ah five? Man, I dunno." "Well, is yo' goin' wit de gals?" "Naw, man, naw." "Well, yo' is fouh!"

With this unfunny story, we hit the ceiling. "Man," someone said, "you ought to know better than that. You ought to have more sense. Why, that story is an insult to every Negro in the world, and you know it damn well."

Friend C was disturbed. He said he didn't see where the joke was harmful, and we didn't take time to explain it to him. Everyone rode him but good. We asked him what he thought he was trying to do at the college, to tear down all we had done? Did he think we would go for his lily-white ideas, his Uncle Tom talk? I must say C did not get sore. Simply took it, and I guess we gave him a load. . . .

I don't know what turned the conversation. We got off on Cox's Marxian point of view, then onto Warner and Myrdal. Argument was even hotter than it had been with C, for our faculty splits wide open. . . . We never agree on anything, unless we have to. . . . C came right along, as if nothing had happened. The meeting got chummy again, breaking up at midnight.

Here was a difficult dilemma, a group of intellectuals bent upon soliloquizing on what the world should be like, how people should treat people, why cautious, calculated action could get nowhere. To preserve their faith in themselves, they had withdrawn from the illogical life about them, escaping its debasing demands. The campus was a cultural island, having no meaningful contact with the white community 'round about, wanting none on the terms offered. While the faculty had accepted College Study goals in theory, they had from the first denied them in practice. The difference was not in fundamental objective, *the abolition of segregation,* the equalization of rights and privileges. It was a methodological issue, whether or not education could be of any help. We were loath to back out of this tangle, for a walk-out teaches very little, so that our decision was to carry on.

The immediate problem was to get these people to talk, to precipitate tensions, clear the air. At times, a quick shock will do this, such as the insulting bus story, yet stress tests of this sort are always risky. If they are used, it should be as a last resort, a final tactic after standard ways of resolving conflict have been tried. Once group catharsis starts, its precipitator must absorb ego thrusts without flinching. He must not become emotionally involved, argue back, or do anything except to keep talk going. He must remember what he is trying to do, how coiled springs unwind. The hardest task is to move out of the target spot, to redirect attention toward integrative action. If the meeting does not end on a friendly note, if everyone does not feel a bit self blaming, then that group may be counted lost so far as its work goes.

The next entry in the diary is interesting. While we shall not quote in detail, the diarist observes that meetings on the following day "went some better," that they were "more worthwhile." At the bull session that evening, it is recorded that Prof L asked C if he "knew any more funny stories and then told him a rip-snorter of a tale." Talk centered on the "liberal" (radical) in race relations. Who is he, why is he, and how did he get that way? Could a society do without him (or any of its leaders) as it changes? What basic functions does each type of leader perform? Are all these functions interrelated? How far dare anyone compromise with principles and not lose integrity as a person? We did not, of course, find final answers to these questions; in truth we are still in search.

INTERGROUP EDUCATION

While such cases are interesting per se, they have been used here for another purpose. They suggest the growing concern of colleges and schools in human relations. To say that this is a new concern is, as history indicates, quite incorrect. It is as old as teaching itself. What is new about it is its present, and growing, intensity, plus the beginnings of specialized training in the group relations field. For a very brief moment or two, I want to talk about an aspect of this field, an area called *intergroup or intercultural education*. This was, of course, the target at which the College Study was directed and it is our hope that study findings will be of use to educators in structuring this teacher training field.

To define a field of study is, first, to locate its center, after which other elements can be fitted in.[2] The center of intergroup education is, we believe, the interactions of majority-minority groups, notably those centering on race, creed, and national origins (immigrant cultures). Other group-to-group relations might be named, for example, labor-management. But omitting all marginal concerns, the field as it is now shaping up can be visualized in a simple diagram.

[2]The present writer, in collaboration with Elaine Forsyth Cook, has prepared a college text, *Intergroup Relations,* to be published by the McGraw-Hill Book Co. in 1953.

Interactions	Time	Place	Social Class
Inter-racial			
Inter-creedal			
Native-alien cultures			

In the chart given, race, creed and immigrant cultures are treated as independent variables, with time, place and social class as dependent, situational factors. The point of stress is intergroup relations, so that two related foci of educational concern should be read into the diagram. One is an interest in intragroup attitudes and behaviors, the other is personality development.

At first glance, one might define "majority-minority" group relations in terms of head count, the former concept meaning over half a population but not all. On further thought, it will be seen that more than *numbers* is involved. "The mere fact," write the Roses, "of being generally hated because of religious, racial or national background is what defines a minority group."[3] It appears to us that hatred is too strong a word, that ingroup attitudes toward outgroup members range from indifference through degrees of dislike to extreme hostility. Moreover, where hatred does exist, it begets hatred. With Group A hating Group B, and Group B reciprocating, illwill does not define either group.

Within every minority, say Negro Americans, Jewish Americans, American Catholics, there is an *ingroup identification,* a complex of attitudes built about own group and other group reactions. Cultural differences, based on race, creed, etc., exist, yet they appear to be of less significance in determining group to group interactions than do two other factors. One is

[3]Arnold and Caroline Rose, *America Divided* (New York: A. A. Knopf, 1948), p. 3.

a *status difference*, with minorities rated as of lower rank order, a lesser breed of people. The other is a *power potential*, the ability to make and/or compel decisions, thus to limit the life chances of all lesser privileged groups. Wherever in the world sociological majorities exist, they are the gatekeepers of cultural opportunities. They open doors or close them to countless cultural goods—to jobs, schooling, health, housing, and the like. In our nation, as elsewhere, minorities are struggling for equal rights and, we hope, equal responsibilities. To further thought and action on these tensional issues is the basic aim of intergroup education.

COLLEGE LEADERSHIP FUNCTION

If the kind of thinking advanced in this lecture, in fact in all the Franklin lectures, should be taught to youth and adults, to professional workers such as school teachers and agency personnel, where should such teaching be lodged? Where, if not in our colleges and universities? To be certain, government will have a big stake in this for it is all-of-us-speaking-for-us-all, in fact every department of society will be involved. Yet it seems reasonable to expect that the institutions of formal education will play a leading role. Here the views of a respected social scientist seem apropos, views expressed at a conference of college officials on the undemocratic college "quota system."

> I reject the view that it is the simple duty of a university to bring together teachers and scholars, each separately teaching and studying what he wants to study or is hired to teach. A university is put there by society, not that each of its professors shall pursue his own interests, but that there shall be a better society. . . . Knowledge is to be sought and taught for the public good. . . .

> The very privileges of academic people, the special opportunities they enjoy, give the university a role of

leadership in the common effort which it would be stupid to ignore and cowardly to refuse. The university, in this view, is not a mere agency of public opinion. It is an institution of moral leadership in the community, and it is to lead toward justice for all.[4]

It is this fact of intellectual and moral leadership which all these lectures have tried to communicate. A college is a peculiar place, a miniature universe. It can reflect the world about it, its confusions and alarms, its expedient ways of treating people, its unconcern for the underdog. Or it can, within limits, assert leadership, give impetus and direction to social change. It can illuminate group life, rather than refract it, become a beacon rather than a mirror of its times. I think we all feel confident as to what the founders of the Franklin Chair in Human Relations, and the public whom it serves, had in mind.

[4]Robert Redfield, "Race and Religion in Selective Admission," *Journal of the American Association of College Registrars,* 21 (1946), 534.